Beyond Ava & Aiden

ALSO BY LINDA ROSENKRANTZ & PAMELA REDMOND SATRAN

Cool Irish Names for Babies

Cool Names

The Baby Name Bible:
The Ultimate Guide by America's Baby-Naming Experts

Beyond Jennifer & Jason, Madison & Montana:
What to Name Your Baby Now

Baby Names Now

Beyond Ava & Aiden

The Enlightened Guide to
Naming Your Baby

LINDA ROSENKRANTZ &
PAMELA REDMOND SATRAN

St. Martin's Griffin
New York

www.stmartins.com

Book design by Michelle McMillian

Library of Congress Cataloging-in-Publication Data

Rosenkrantz, Linda.
    Beyond Ava & Aiden : the enlightened guide to naming your baby / Linda Rosenkrantz & Pamela Redmond Satran.—1st ed.
        p. cm.
    Includes index.
    ISBN-13: 978-0-312-53915-3
    ISBN-10: 0-312-53915-0
    1. Names, Personal—United States—Handbooks, manuals, etc.
    2. Infants—United States—Miscellanea.   I. Satran, Pamela Redmond.
II. Title.   III. Title: Beyond Ava and Aiden.
    CS2377.R6648   2008
    929.4'4—dc22   2009007366

First Edition: July 2009

10 9 8 7 6 5 4 3 2 1

For the wonderful daughters and sons we've named . . .

Chloe Samantha,

Rory Elizabeth Margaret,

Joseph Leopold,

and Owen Redmond

Contents

Acknowledgments

We would like to extend our warmest thanks to our brilliant editor, Hope Dellon, who has been providing us with both perspicacious editorial advice and friendship since the very first edition of *Beyond Jennifer & Jason*. Also at St. Martin's, we have had support in putting together and promoting our books from Laura Bourgeois, Anne Marie Tallberg, and Rachel Ekstrom. We want to take this opportunity, too, to acknowledge our terrific nameberry team: Hugh Hunter, Ed Sim, and Jefferson Rabb, and to the others who have provided such valuable help—Betsy Rosini, Danielle Miksza, Kimberly Caputo, Neil Rosini, Rita DiMatteo, and Steve Adamczyk.

And finally, we'd like to thank all the parents who have listened to us talk about names all these years and who now freely share their own enlightened thoughts with us.

Introduction

What happened to Jennifer and Jason, the names behind the name of our very first book? They're all grown up and naming babies of their own now, and so it's time for a new baby-name guide for the next generation: *Beyond Ava & Aiden*.

Beyond Jennifer & Jason inspired a baby-naming revolution that transformed what and how millions of parents name their children. Rather than reaching for the handiest family name or trendy favorite, parents now invest tremendous time and energy in choosing the perfect name for their baby. They're well aware of the power of a name to influence how people see their child. And they're way more adventurous than their own parents were, considering names that defy old gender stereotypes, that push through international boundaries, that carry deep personal meaning, and show off their own individual style.

Of course, the Internet has changed the way people search for names, making it enormously more efficient to hunt down a name that meets all your requirements: One that works for girls as well as boys, that means something related to nature, and that's Irish, for instance. You can accomplish that on our own Web site, nameberry.com, much more efficiently than you can with any book.

But to truly make the best name choice for your baby, you need the kind of comprehensive information and in-depth expertise contained in *Beyond Ava & Aiden*. As much fun as it can be to chat about names online, no other newbie parent is going to be able to offer the level of knowledge and advice you'll find here. And no amount of analyzing the popularity statistics on the Web will give you the kind of foresight and analysis you need to pick a name that's right for you now and will still feel right for your child over a lifetime.

Beyond Ava & Aiden is filled with hundreds of the kind of subjective lists we invented, telling you what's cool, what's hot, and what's overheated, which names are hipster and which are Harvard-bound. This book offers you girly-girl names, names for your little dude, and names that work best for twins. We present undiscovered names from Tibet, chic names from Paris, and names fit for a baby god or goddess.

Each list is supported by the kind of information today's smart baby namer craves: where trends come from and where they're going. What psychologists say about the effect of unusual names and how much a name influences a child's chance of success. Whether unisex names work as well for boys as for girls and what you should know about nicknames, middle names, and sibling names.

All the information you need to choose the kind of name you and your child will love forever is organized into four easy-to-follow sections:

STYLE: A look at baby-naming fashion and trends: What's in, out, hot, not. We analyze which names are most fashionable right now and why, including A+ names that may encourage kids to get better grades, names that have just been invented, and names inspired by celebrities. We also offer a cautionary list of names that are becoming too faddish, substitutes you might consider, plus hundreds of undiscovered names we predict will come into style over the next decades.

IMAGE: A guide to the impressions names make: which names sound hip, serious, creative, and classy. This section includes detailed information on how a name's image affects your child, which names are moving up and down the class ladder, and how to choose a name that offers the perfect balance between fitting in and standing out.

SEX: Gender lines are constantly being redrawn, and here we help you mark them. Girls' names are divided into four main categories: Girly-Girl, Womanly, Girlish, and Boyish. Boys' names are classed as Power-boys, All-Boy Classics, Biblical Boys, and Metrodudes. And then we detail the Unisex names, more appropriate than ever for both boys and girls, and the starbabies who promote them.

TRADITION: A look at names over history, around the world, and within cultural and religious groups. Here's where you'll find fascinating Jewish, Muslim, and saints' names, undiscovered choices fashionable in Europe, and how to pick a name that reflects your unique background. Also here: how to choose a name you and your spouse both love, how to deal with lame name advice, and why you should name your baby with future siblings in mind.

Beyond Ava & Aiden can be used as a companion to our other best-selling name guides, our comprehensive baby-naming dictionary *The Baby Name Bible* and our edgier *Cool Names for Babies,* as well as our Web site, nameberry.com. But it can also stand on its own as a way to both explore the newest, hippest names and to gather the sort of authoritative information you need for your baby-naming research.

In the end, after reading this book, you'll know you made the very best name choice possible for your child, whether you decide to move beyond Ava and Aiden or not.

Style

Style is the most important consideration for many parents when choosing a name. But how to factor current naming trends into a choice that lasts forever? How do you balance fashion dictates with your own personal style, and when do other considerations like image and family take precedence?

In this section, we help you untangle the hows, whys, and whats of the baby-name style decision by showing you which names are hot right now, which are coming into style, and which are fading away.

The Hot Names, those that are being favored by large numbers of parents at the moment, include gently old-fashioned Vintage Names and newly hatched Millennials, names inspired by celebrities and names that may motivate your child to get straight As! If you're looking for a name that reflects the most current style, here's where to look.

Parents who hate the idea of choosing an overly trendy name can be guided by our list of names that are So Far In They're Out. But don't despair if you do find your personal favorite there: we also offer worthy substitutes for overplayed choices.

And if you'd rather lead the trends instead of follow them, we offer hundreds of new names—from the Green to the Godlike to the So-Uncool-They're-Cool—to propel you into the future of baby naming.

What's Hot

A+ NAMES

Today's baby namers not only want their kids to get As later on in school, they want to give them an A to start off with—as the initial letter of their names. There's been a remarkable upsurge of hot *A* names—we did, after all, call this book *Beyond Ava & Aiden*—especially if you consider that in 1975 only seven of the top fifty names began with *any* vowel, while in 2007 there were seventeen beginning just with the letter *A*. Vowel names in general are on the rise—lots of interesting *E*, *I*, and *O* names as well—but *A* as in Alpha is definitely the leader of the pack.

And there are even some scientific grounds for choosing an *A* name. A study by Leif Nelson of the University of California, San Diego, and Joseph Simmons of Yale in the journal *Psychological Science* stated that students whose names began with *A* or *B* earned higher averages than students whose names began with letters farther down the alphabet, and that there were also more students in top-ranking law schools with names starting with *A* or *B*—so making an A-pick now might just help point your child toward the A-list.

You'll find lots more *A* names plus other vowel-beginning names on the other hot and cool lists. But here are some of the hottest *A* names:

Girls

AALIYAH	ANGEL
ABIGAIL	ANGELICA
ADA	ANGELINA
ADDIE/ADDY	ANIKA/ANNIKA
ADDISON	ANNA
ADELAIDE	ANNABEL(LA)
ADELINE	ANOUK
ADRIANA	ANYA
AERIN	APHRA
AINSLEY	APPLE
AISLINN (ASH-LIN)	ARABELLA
ALABAMA	ARAMINTA
ALEXA	ARDEN
ALEXIA	ARIA
ALEXIS	ARIAN(N)A
ALI	ARMANI
ALICE	ARTEMIS
ALLEGRA	ASHA
ALMA	ASHBY
AMABEL	ASHLYN
AMELIA	ASIA
AMELIE	ASPEN
AMERICA	AUBREY
AMITY	AUDEN
ANAÏS	AUDREY
ANASTASIA	AUGUSTA
ANDROMEDA	AUTUMN
	AVA

AVALON

AVALYN/AVELINE

AVERY

AVIS

Boys

AARON

ABBOTT

ACE

ACHILLES

ADAIR

ADRIAN

AIDAN/AIDEN

ALESSANDRO

ALEX

ALFIE

AMORY

ANDERSON

ANGEL

ANGUS

APOLLO

ARCHER

ARI

ARMANI

ARROW

ARTHUR

ASA

ASH

ASHER

ASHTON

ATTICUS

AUDEN

AUGUST

AUGUSTEN/AUGUSTIN

AXEL

AZARIAH

MILLENNIAL NAMES

There is an entire generation of names moving rapidly up the popularity list that distinguish themselves by being newly minted. Even if they existed as surnames or place names or occupations, they've rarely been used before as first names. Many of them are morphed versions of names that were used in another form earlier, while others have been spun from thin air.

The underlying feeling seems to be a desire for a new beginning along with the new millennium. Anything we did and said, felt and experienced in the last century is over now. We've entered an era of change, and these names are evidence of that belief.

Girls (mostly)

ADDISON
AINSLEY
ARIA
AVERY
BROOKLYN
CADENCE
CALI
CHEYENNE
ELLE
HARLOW
LEXI
MACY
MARLEY
MYA
REESE
SAGE
SAILOR
SCOUT
SIENNA
SIERRA
SKYLA
SKYLAR
TAYLA
TRISTA

Boys (mostly)

ASH
ASHTON
BECKETT
BRADEN

BRADY
BRAXTON
BRYSON
CADE
CALE
CAMDEN
CANNON
CHACE
CHANCE
COLBY
COLT
COLTON
DARWIN
DAWSON
EASTON
FISHER
FLINT
GABLE
GAGE
GRAYSON
HUDSON
HUNTER
JADEN
JAX
JAXON
JET
JETSON
KANE
KIAN
KYLAN
KYLER

LANDON	FINLAY
LENNON	HARLEY
LENNOX	JALEN
LOGAN	JAMESON
MAVERICK	JUSTICE
ORION	KAI
ROCKET	KEATON
RYDER	KENNEDY
STEEL	LONDON
STONE	PAYTON/PEYTON
TRENTON	REEVE
ZANDER	RILEY
	ROMY
Either	ROWAN
AUDEN	SAWYER
BLAZE	TAJ
DEVON	TRACE

New-Age Names

Related to the Millennial group are the New-Age Names—children of the new era but with a distinctly spiritual twist. These names reflect positivity, peace, an enduring strength and the thirst for a higher power. They include:

ANGEL	DESTINY
ANSWER	DEVA
BLISS	DHARMA
BODHI	EDEN
CHARITY	ESSENCE
DEACON	EVER

FAITH	PATIENCE
GENESIS	PAX
HARMONY	PAXTON
HAVEN	PEACE
HEAVEN	PRAISE
HONOR	SERENITY
INFINITY	TRINITY
JUSTICE	TRUE
MERCY	TRUTH
MESSIAH	VERITY
MIRACLE	ZEN
NEVAEH	ZION

STAR POWER

The names of stars and their children are flashed before the public all day, every day, and not just in the gossip magazines and TV shows and online blogs, but on the national nightly news and in mainstream media like the *New York Times*, *Time*, and *Newsweek*. Those famous names have become an increasingly powerful influence on baby-naming trends in general and on what we name our individual children. A star can single-handedly make a boy's name like Drew or Cameron seem feminine and sexy, catapult a shy old favorite like Violet or Matilda to superstardom, even raise an old-school glamorous name like Ava or Harlow from the dead. Celebrities have made us more accepting of quirky ethnic names such as Viggo and Suri, have encouraged us to look for names that honor significant places (Kingston) or heroes (Nouvel), and have inspired us to invent unique names—from Beyoncé to January to Story—of our very own.

Starbabies

When your great-aunt Agnes can reel off all twelve first and middle names of the Jolie-Pitt sextet, you know you're living in a culture that celebrates celebrity babies. We scrutinize their high-profile moms' bumps, pore over their nurseries and layettes, and when the name is finally announced, everyone weighs in: Is it too far out? Is it too trendy? Will it work in my neighborhood as well as it works in Malibu?

Many of the names below have either already become hot or are beginning to heat up thanks to a starbaby's influence. A star can pluck a name out of limbo and give it new life and potential, as in the cases of Julia Roberts's Hazel (not a popular choice at first), Tina Fey's Alice, Jessica Alba's Honor, and several celebrities' picks of Tallulah. The same holds true for boys, with such instant hits as Kingston (Rossdale), Maddox (Jolie-Pitt), and several Becketts. Even older children thrust in the spotlight—most notably, Malia and Sasha Obama—can inspire real-life namesakes.

The following is a selective list of starbaby choices that might influence your pick for the newest star in your own family:

Girls

AGNES	Elisabeth Shue & Davis Guggenheim
ALABAMA	Drea de Matteo & Shooter Jennings
ALICE	Tina Fey, Tom Cavanaugh
ANGEL	Melanie (Spice Girl) Brown
APPLE	Gwyneth Paltrow & Chris Martin
ARIZONA	Art (Everclear) Alexakis
ASHBY	Nancy O'Dell
AUDREY	Greg Kinnear
AVA	Kevin Dillon, Mia Hamm & Nomar Garciaparra, Jason Priestley, Caroline Rhea—to name the most recent
AVALON	Rena Sofer

AVIS	Daniel Baldwin
BAILEY	Scott Baio, Stella McCartney, Teri Polo
	(who spelled it Bayley)
BIRDIE	Busy Philipps
BLUEBELL	Geri (Spice Girl) Halliwell
BRIGHTON	Jon Favreau
CHARLESTON	Joey Lawrence
CHARLIE	Rebecca Romijn & Jerry O'Connell
CLEMENTINE	Ethan Hawke
COCO	Courteney Cox & David Arquette
DOLLY	Rebecca Romijn & Jerry O'Connell
DOMINO	India Hicks
EASTON	Elisabeth Röhm
EDEN	Marcia Cross
EDIE	Samantha Morton
EMERY	Angie Harmon & Jason Sehorn
EVER	Milla Jovovich & Paul Anderson
FINLEY	Lisa Marie Presley
GIA	Matt Damon
GRIER	Brooke Shields
HARLOW	Nicole Richie & Joel Madden
HARPER	Martie (Dixie Chick) Maguire, Lisa Marie Presley
HEAVEN	Brooke Burke
HONOR	Jessica Alba & Cash Warren
INDIGO	Lou Diamond Phillips
JAGGER	Soleil Moon Frye
JOHNNIE	Melissa Etheridge
JUNO	Will (Coldplay) Champion
LOTUS	Rain Pryor
LUNA	Constance Marie
MAEVE	Chris O'Donnell

MARLO	Rob Corddry
MARS	Erykah Badu & Jay Electronica
MERCY	Andy Richter
MILEY	Rev Run
NAHLA	Halle Berry
NAVY	Nivea & Terius Nash
NELL	Helena Bonham Carter & Tim Burton
ODETTE	Mark Ruffalo
OLIVE	Isla Fisher & Sacha Baron Cohen
PALOMA	David Caruso
PETAH	Ani DiFranco
PIPER	Samantha Bee
RHIANNON	Robert Rodriguez
ROMY	Sofia Coppola
RUBY	Tobey Maguire, Charlotte Church
SADIE	Adam Sandler, Finola Hughes
SAGE	Toni Collette
SAM	Tiger Woods
SAWYER	Sara Gilbert
SCARLETT	Karen Elson & Jack (White Stripes) White
SERAPHINA	Jennifer Garner & Ben Affleck
SHILOH	Angelina Jolie & Brad Pitt
SIENNA	Campbell Brown
STELLA	Tori Spelling
SUNDAY	Nicole Kidman & Keith Urban
SURI	Katie Holmes & Tom Cruise
TALLULAH	Philip Seymour Hoffman, Damon Dash
TRUE	Joely Fisher
VALENTINA	Selma Hayek
VIOLET	Jennifer Garner & Ben Affleck, Dave (Foo Fighters) Grohl

VIVIENNE	Angelina Jolie & Brad Pitt
WILLA	Philip Seymour Hoffman
ZAHARA	Angelina Jolie & Brad Pitt

Boys

ACE	Tom (No Doubt) Dumont, Jennie Finch & Casey Daigle
ARCHIBALD	Amy Poehler & Will Arnett
ATTICUS	Summer Phoenix & Casey Affleck
AUGUST	Mariska Hargitay
AUGUSTIN	Linda Evangelista
BECKETT	Stella McCartney, Conan O'Brien, Diane Farr
CALLUM	Kyle MacLachlan
CASH	Joshua Morrow, Annabeth Gish
COLT	Cole Hauser
CRUZ	Victoria & David Beckham
DARBY	Patrick Dempsey
DEACON	Reese Witherspoon & Ryan Phillippe, Don Johnson
DEXTER	Diana Krall & Elvis Costello, Charlotte Church
DEZI	Jaime Pressly
EVERLY	Anthony (Red Hot Chili Peppers) Kiedis
FELIX	Gillian Anderson
FINLEY	Chris O'Donnell
FINN	Christy Turlington & Ed Burns
FLETCHER	Samantha Bee
GABLE	Kevin Nealon
GIANNI	Jill Hennessy
GIDEON	Ziggy Marley
GULLIVER	Damian Lewis
HAYES	Kevin Costner

IGNATIUS	Cate Blanchett, Julianne Nicholson
JAGGER	Lindsay Davenport
KIERAN	Julianna Margulies
KINGSTON	Gwen Stefani & Gavin Rossdale
KNOX	Angelina Jolie & Brad Pitt
LEVI	Camila Alves & Matthew McConaughey
LUCA	Vincent D'Onofrio
MADDOX	Angelina Jolie & Brad Pitt, McKenzie Westmore
MAGNUS	Will Ferrell, Kristy Swanson
MALACHY	Cillian Murphy
MAX	Christina Aguilera
MAXIMILIAN	Jennifer Lopez & Marc Anthony
MILLER	Melissa Etheridge
MOSES	Gwyneth Paltrow & Chris Martin
ORION	Chris Noth
ORSON	Paz Vega, Lauren Ambrose
OSCAR	Gillian Anderson
PAX	Angelina Jolie & Brad Pitt
REX	Will (Coldplay) Champion
RIO	Tom (No Doubt) Dumont
RIVER	Keri Russell
ROMEO	Victoria & David Beckham
SLATER	Angela Bassett & Courtney B. Vance
STORY	Jenna Elfman
SULLIVAN	Patrick Dempsey
TENNYSON	Russell Crowe
THEO	Bryce Dallas Howard
VIGGO	Taylor Hanson
WINSTON	Billie Piper

(See also Nicknamed Starbabies, page 31.)

Apples are so sweet and they're wholesome, and it's biblical. And I just thought it sounded so lovely and clean.

—Gwyneth Paltrow, mother of Apple and Moses

There's nothing weird about calling your baby Chewbacca if that's what you want to call your baby. It's no stranger than Sarah. A name is just a noise, and if you like it, then [expletive] what everyone else says.

—Chris Martin, father of Apple and Moses

The Craziest Starbaby Names

Celebrity baby names don't always prove inspirational for real people. Not many Apples have fallen far from the Paltrow-Martin tree, for instance, and Moxie CrimeFighter will surely be the only one in her class.

Here, some of the craziest starbaby names of recent years, with a "don't try this at home" warning.

Girls

APPLE	Gwyneth Paltrow & Chris Martin
BLUEBELL MADONNA	Geri (Spice Girl) Halliwell
HAPPY	Macy Gray
MAKENA'LEI	Helen Hunt
MOXIE CRIMEFIGHTER	Penn Jillette
PRINCESS TIAAMII	Jordan & Peter Andre

Boys

BANJO	Rachel Griffiths
BRONX MOWGLI	Ashlee Simpson & Pete Wentz
BUSTER	Michele Hicks & Jonny Lee Miller
CROIX	Cedric the Entertainer
DIEZEL	Toni Braxton

HUCKLEBERRY	Bear Grylls
KAL-EL	Nicolas Cage
MARMADUKE	Bear Grylls
NAKOA-WOLF	Lisa Bonet & Jason Momoa
PEANUT	Ingo (*General Hospital*) Rademacher
PHINNAEUS	Julia Roberts
PILOT INSPEKTOR	Jason Lee
PTOLEMY	Gretchen Mol
ROCKET	Robert Rodriguez
SUNNY BEBOP	Michael "Flea" Balzey
ZEPPELIN	Jonathan (Korn) Davis
ZOLTEN	Penn Jillette
ZUMA NESTA ROCK	Gwen Stefani & Gavin Rossdale

Celebrity Inspiration

Along with their babies, more and more celebrities today have names that are unusual, cool, attractive, distinctive. Some of these star-inspired names—Hayden, Sienna, Scarlett, Chace, Anderson—have already inspired what we're naming our babies, and the others here are sure to follow. And even if the world doesn't end up with thousands of baby Beyoncés, the effect of these names is to make us reach harder to find one that's special—starworthy—to launch our own babies into the world. Our hot list:

Female

ALANIS Morrisette
AMERICA Ferrera
AMERIE
ANANDA Lewis
ANGELINA Jolie
ANNIKA Sorenstam

ARDEN Wohl
ASHANTI
AUDRINA Patridge
AVRIL Lavigne
AZURA Skye
BEYONCÉ Knowles
BLAKE Lively

BLU (b. Tiffany) Cantrell

CALISTA Flockhart

CAMERON Diaz

CAMPBELL Brown

CHAN Marshall

CHARISMA Carpenter

CHINA Chow

CHLOE Sevigny

CLEA DuVall

DANICA Patrick

DIDO

DIVA Zappa

DREW Barrymore

ELISHA Cuthbert

EVANGELINE Lilly

FEIST

FERGIE

GISELE Bundchen

HAYDEN Panettiere

IONE Skye

ISLA Fisher

IVANKA Trump

JACINDA Barrett

JADA Pinkett-Smith

JANUARY Jones

Angelina JOLIE

JORJA Fox

KEIRA Knightley

LAKE Bell

LEIGHTON Meester

LIBERTY Ross

MARIAH Carey

MILEY Cyrus

MISCHA Barton

MONET Mazur

MYA

NEVE Campbell

PAZ Vega

PINK

PLUM Sykes

POPPY Montgomery

RIHANNA

RUMER Willis

SAFFRON Burroughs

SAOIRSE Ronan

SCARLETT Johansson

SERENA Williams

SHAKIRA (b. Isabel)

SIENNA Miller

SUNSHINE Tutt

THANDIE Newton

TILA Tequila

TINSLEY Mortimer

TRISTA Sutter

TYRA Banks

VENUS Williams

ZOOEY Deschanel

Male

ADRIAN Grenier

ANDERSON Cooper

ASHTON Kutcher

CHACE Crawford

CILLIAN Murphy

DANE Cook

DAX Shepard

DJIMON Hounsou

ELI Manning

EWAN McGregor

JET Li

JOAQUIN Phoenix

JUDE Law

KANYE West

LEBRON James

LEONARDO DiCaprio

ORLANDO Bloom

PEYTON Manning

RAINN Wilson

ROMANY Malco

SACHA Baron Cohen

SHIA LaBeouf

STELLAN Skarsgård

TIGER Woods

VIGGO Mortensen

WENTWORTH Miller

> After 19 years of getting into fights over his name and hearing it mispronounced, Shia LaBeouf can't believe celebrities are still coming up with weird names for their kids . . . Asked what he would say to parents planning to give their kids strange names, LeBeouf says, "Name your kid Billy and Timmy. What is the problem with that?"
>
> —The Associated Press

Glamour Girls & Boys

But you don't have to be young and hot—or even alive, for that matter—to be a name-influential celebrity: a rich source of new names is old Hollywood history. As attested to by the title of this book, Ava, namesake of breathtakingly beautiful 1940s–50s movie siren Ava Gardner, is one of the most popular names in the country, with the strong potential of reaching Number One. In this case it was celebrity building on celebrity—by our count no fewer than a dozen stars (the first was Aidan Quinn in 1989), from Reese Witherspoon to Hugh Jackman to Martina McBride have bestowed the name on their daughters, polishing up the image of a name that had been moldering in the fusty, musty Ada-Ida-

Edna closet. Not far behind Ava is Audrey, as in Audrey Hepburn, charming and unique beauty, sophisticated fashion icon, and humanitarian. And lately they've been joined by blond bombshell Jean Harlow's surname, picked most recently by Nicole Richie and Joel Madden, and sure to spread like wildfire. Some other currently favored baby names also reverberate with the echoes of past star power. Grace, for example, suggests the cool, elegant blond beauty of Grace Kelly, and the megapopular Sophia conjures up the sultry Italian image of Sophia Loren.

What are some other possibilities to join this stellar group? Here are a few ideas from the Golden and Silver Ages of Hollywood.

Female

ANOUK Aimée
BRIGITTE Bardot
CLAUDETTE Colbert
GINGER Rogers
GREER Garson
GRETA Garbo
HEDY Lamarr
INGRID Bergman
LANA Turner
LENA Horne
LIV Ullman
MAE West
MAMIE Van Doren
MARLENE (pronounced mar-LAY-na) Dietrich
MERLE Oberon
MIA Farrow
NATALIE Wood

OLIVIA DeHavilland
PAULETTE Goddard
PIPER Laurie
RITA Hayworth
ROMY Schneider
ROSALIND Russell
SIMONE Signoret
TALLULAH Bankhead
URSULA Andress
VERONICA Lake
VIVEKA Lindfors
VIVIEN Leigh

Male

(for several of these, it's the surname that's the winner)
Gene AUTRY
Marlon BRANDO
James CAGNEY

Gary COOPER	OMAR Sharif
Bing CROSBY	ORSON Welles
MARCELLO Mastroianni	REX Harrison
Joel McCREA	RORY Calhoun
NOEL Coward	SPENCER Tracy
Laurence OLIVIER	VAN Johnson

Opting for a solo one-word stage name is like grabbing for the brass ring in celebritydom. It's a naked bid for icon status, a way to brand yourself like Kleenex or Xerox or Liberace.

—Rachel Abramowitz, *Los Angeles Times*

NAMES THAT WORK

Have you noticed how many of the boys' names climbing up the ladder end in the letters *er*? They sound really new and cool, but a large proportion of them actually originated in medieval England as occupational surnames, when Timothy the Tanner morphed into Timothy Tanner—as if in our day Pete the Programmer became Pete Programmer. And even if many of these trades no longer exist in this Digital Age and some of their meanings have been lost to time, part of their appeal lies in their throwback reference to basic concepts of honest labor, giving them more historical heft than other fashionable two-syllable names. They offer the parents of boy babies a comfortable middle ground between the sharper-edged single-syllable names (Holt, Colt), and the more ornate longer names (Gregory, Jeremy) of the recent past. Some of them, like Cooper, Harper, and Hunter, have been in use for a while, but there are other, more unusual ones just waiting to be discovered. Here are the most usable, with their original, sometimes arcane, meanings.

The *Er*-ending Names

ARCHER professional bowman

BAKER baker

BANNER flag bearer

BARBER at one time barbers also did surgery and dentistry

BARKER stripper of bark from trees for tanning

BAXTER baker, usually female

BEAMER trumpet player

BOOKER scribe

BOYER bow maker, cattle herder

BRENNER charcoal burner

BREWER/BREWSTER brewer of beer

BRIDGER builder of bridges

CARDEN wool carder

CARTER cart maker or driver, transporter of goods

CARVER sculptor

CHANDLER candle maker

CHAUCER maker of breeches, boots, or leg armor

COLLIER charcoal seller, coal miner

CONNER inspector

COOPER wooden barrel maker

COSTER fruit grower or seller

CURRIER leather finisher

CUTLER knife maker

DECKER roofer

DEXTER dyer

DRAPER woolen cloth maker or seller

DUFFER peddler

FARRIER ironworker

FISHER fisherman

FLETCHER arrow maker

FORESTER gamekeeper, forest warden

FOSTER sheep shearer

FOWLER hunter of wild birds

GARDNER gardener

GLOVER maker or seller of gloves

GRANGER granary worker

HARPER harp maker or player

HOOPER one who makes or fits hoops for barrels

HOPPER dancer, acrobat

HUNTER huntsman

JAGGER peddler, usually of fish

KEELER barge maker

KIEFER barrel maker

LANDER launderer

LARDNER servant in charge of the larder

LORIMER spur maker

MERCER merchant, especially in luxury fabrics

MILLER grinder of corn

NAYLER maker of nails

PAINTER self-explanatory

PARKER gamekeeper in a medieval private park

PORTER gatekeeper, carrier of goods

POTTER maker or seller of earthenware pottery

QUILLER scribe

RANGER game warden

RIDER/RYDER cavalryman, horseman, messenger

SADLER saddle maker

SALTER worker in or seller of salt

SAWYER woodsman, carpenter

SAYER assayer of metal, food taster

SCHUYLER scholar, teacher

SLATER roofer

SPENCER a dispenser of provisions

SUMNER court summoner

TANNER processor of animal skins for leather

THATCHER roofer

TOLLIVER metalworker

TUCKER cloth worker, fabric pleater

TURNER turner of wood on a lathe

TYLER worker with roof tiles

WALKER worker in cloth, cloth walker

WEBSTER weaver, originally female

I was thinking of naming my kid Doctor if I have one. Doctor Fallon. Then whatever he does, he's set.

—Jimmy Fallon

Other Occupational Names

BAILEY bailiff or other administrator

BAIRD minstrel or poet

BARLEY grower or seller of barley

BEAMAN beekeeper

CHAPIN clergyman

CLARK clerk, cleric, or scholar

DEACON church dignitary

FARRAR blacksmith, metalworker

FISK fisherman

JUDGE self-explanatory

MARSHALL one who looked after horses, later ceremonial official

MASON skilled stoneworker

PARSON rector

PILOT ship pilot

REEVE bailiff, chief magistrate

SAILOR sailor

SHEPHERD herder of
sheep

SHERMAN trimmer of the nap
of cloth after weaving

SMITH metalworker, blacksmith

STEELE steelworker

TAYLOR cutter of clothes, tailor

TODD fox hunter

TRAVIS gatekeeper, toll collector

WARD watchman, guard

WRIGHT carpenter, joiner

VINTAGE CHIC

Brides these days are wearing vintage gowns, fashionistas are searching for vintage purses and shoes. But it's not shabby chic we're talking about anymore, or frilly Victorian-period remnants: Vintage now has moved on to sleeker, more stylish, classic—preferably designer—pieces from the last few decades. And it's similarly true of names. Today's parents looking for a vintage name are less likely to consider the fussy Victorian valentines that were revived in the eighties—good-bye Marissa, Melissa, Cassandra, and Clarissa—than to opt for a simpler, more-modern-sounding oldie. These are names that had gone out of fashion and been passed over for a few decades, but which still make solid choices, with harder consonants and stronger vowels. Here are some prime examples:

Girls
ADELINE

ALICE

AMELIA

AUDREY

AVA

BEATRICE

BELLA

CELIA

CHARLOTTE

CLAIRE

CLARA

CLAUDIA

CLEMENTINE

CORA

CORNELIA

DAISY

EDITH

ELEANOR

ELIZA

ELLA

EMMA

ESMÉ

EUGENIA

EVA

EVE

EVELYN

FAITH

FAY

FLORA

FRANCES

GEORGIA

~~GRACE~~

GRETA

HAZEL

HELEN

HONOR

HOPE

IMOGEN

IRIS

ISABEL

IVY

JANE

JOSEPHINE

JULIA

JULIET

JUNE

LILA

LILY

LOUISA

LUCY

MADELINE

MATILDA

MAUDE

MAY

MIRANDA

NATALIE

NINA

NORA

OLIVE

OLIVIA

PATIENCE

PAULINE

PEARL

PHOEBE

POLLY

RAMONA

ROSALIND

ROSE

RUBY

SOPHIA

SOPHIE

STELLA
SYLVIA
VERONICA
VIOLET
VIVIAN
WILLA

Boys
ABBOTT
ABRAHAM
ASHER
CALEB
CALVIN
DUNCAN
EDISON
ELI
ELIJAH
ELLIOT
EMMETT
EPHRAIM
ETHAN
EVERETT
EZRA
FELIX
FRANCIS
GEORGE
GIDEON
HARRY
HENRY
HOMER
HORATIO

ISAAC
JACK
JARED
~~JASPER~~
JONAH
JONAS
JOSIAH
JUDAH
JULIAN
LEO
LEVI
LINCOLN
LOWELL
LUCAS
LUCIAN
MAX
MICAH
MILES
MOSES
NATHAN
NATHANIEL
NED
NOAH
OLIVER
ORSON
OSCAR
OWEN
PATRICK
QUINCY
SAMSON
SEBASTIAN

SIMON

SPENCER

THEO

TOBIAS

TRUMAN

WALTER

WARD

WILL

XAVIER

Vintage Starbabies

Girls

ALICE	Tina Fey, Tom Cavanaugh
AMELIA	Lisa Rinna & Harry Hamlin
AUDREY	Greg Kinnear, Faith Hill & Tim McGraw
AVA	Reese Witherspoon & Ryan Phillippe, Kevin Dillon, Hugh Jackman, Caroline Rhea, Martina McBride, and several others
BEATRICE	Paul McCartney
BELLA	Mark Ruffalo, Billy Bob Thornton, Eddie Murphy, and others
CHARLOTTE	Dylan McDermott, Embeth Davidtz, Amy Brenneman, Harry Connick, Jr.
CLAIRE	Albert Brooks
CLAUDIA	Michelle Pfeiffer
CLEMENTINE	Claudia Schiffer, Ethan Hawke
DAISY	Meg Ryan, Jamie Oliver
ELEANOR	Diane Lane
ELLA	Annette Bening & Warren Beatty, Kelly Preston & John Travolta, Eric Clapton, Ben Stiller, Mark Wahlberg, Jeff Gordon, and others
EMMA	Wayne Gretzky, Kristi Yamaguchi
ESMÉ	Samantha Morton, Anthony Edwards

FAITH	Rick Schroder
FRANCES	Amanda Peet, Kate Spade
GRACE	Lance Armstrong, Mia Hamm, Norah O'Donnell, Elisabeth & Tim Hasselbeck, and others
GRETA	David Caruso, Phoebe Cates & Kevin Kline
HAZEL	Julia Roberts
HONOR	Jessica Alba, Tilda Swinton
HOPE	Brad Garrett
IRIS	Sadie Frost & Jude Law
ISABEL	Annette Bening & Warren Beatty, Stanley Tucci, Angela Kinsey
ISABELLA	Matt Damon, Drew Lachey, Sean Astin, Josh Gracin, and others
JOSEPHINE	Vera Wang
JULIET	Emily Watson
LILA	Kate Moss
LILY	Lisa Hartman & Clint Black, Greg Kinnear
LUCY	Laura Leighton, Nancy Grace
MATILDA	Michelle Williams & Heath Ledger, Molly Ringwald, Moon Unit Zappa
NELL	Helena Bonham Carter & Tim Burton
NINA	"Weird Al" Yankovic
OLIVE	Isla Fisher & Sacha Baron Cohen
OLIVIA	Justine Bateman, Eddie Vedder, Beverly D'Angelo & Al Pacino
PEARL	Maya Rudolph & Paul Thomas Anderson
PHOEBE	Bill Gates
RAMONA	Maggie Gyllenhaal & Peter Sarsgaard
RUBY	Tobey Maguire, Charlotte Church
SADIE	Adam Sandler

SERAPHINA	Jennifer Garner & Ben Affleck
SOPHIA	Soledad O'Brien, Talisa Soto & Benjamin Bratt
SOPHIE	Luke Perry
STELLA	Melanie Griffith & Antonio Banderas, Tori Spelling, Peri Gilpin
VERONICA	Rebecca De Mornay & Patrick O'Neal
VIOLET	Jennifer Garner & Ben Affleck, Dave Grohl
WILLA	Philip Seymour Hoffman

Boys

ARCHIBALD	Amy Poehler & Will Arnett
ASHER	Embeth Davidtz
CALEB	Julianne Moore, Bo Bice
DEXTER	Diana Krall & Elvis Costello, Charlotte Church
ELI	Campbell Brown
ELIJAH	Bono, Donnie Wahlberg
ETHAN	Edward Furlong
EZRA	Paul Reiser
FELIX	Gillian Anderson
FLETCHER	Samantha Bee
FRANK	Diana Krall & Elvis Costello
FREDERICK	Mayim Bialik
GEORGE	Kristin Scott Thomas, Eva Herzigova
GIDEON	Ziggy Marley
HARRY	David Letterman
HENRY	Julia Roberts, Heidi Klum & Seal, Norah O'Donnell, Emily Robison, Rachel Weisz, Steve Zahn, Minnie Driver, and others
HOMER	Carey Lowell & Richard Gere, Anne Heche
IGNATIUS	Cate Blanchett

JACK	Matt Lauer, Joan Lunden, Christie Brinkley, and several others
JASPER	Wynton Marsalis, Don Johnson
JONAS	Tom DeLonge
JUDAH	Lucy Lawless
JULIAN	Jessica Sklar & Jerry Seinfeld, Lisa Kudrow
LEO	Kim Raver
LEVI	Matthew McConaughey, Sara Gilbert
LINCOLN	Bill Murray
LUCIAN	Steve Buscemi
MILES	Joan Cusack, Larenz Tate
MOSES	Gwyneth Paltrow & Chris Martin
NATHAN	Jon Stewart
NOAH	Scott Weiland, Kim Alexis
OLIVER	Bridget Fonda & Danny Elfman, Fred Savage, Taylor Hawkins
ORSON	Paz Vega, Lauren Ambrose
OSCAR	Gillian Anderson, Hugh Jackman
OWEN	Noah Wyle, Ricki Lake
REX	Will (Coldplay) Champion
SEBASTIAN	Kim Fields, James Spader
SPENCER	Gena Lee Nolan
TRUMAN	Rita Wilson & Tom Hanks
WALTER	Rainn Wilson
WILL	Wendy Wilson, Meg Tilly & Colin Firth
XAVIER	Tilda Swinton, Donnie Wahlberg

JUST JOSIES

We're living in an ever-more-casual, informal society. The stranger who calls us up to ask for a charitable contribution assumes we're on a first-name basis. Kids are more likely to call the parents of their friends Scott and Stephanie than they are Mr. and Mrs. Miller, and in many schools students are encouraged to address their teachers by their first names. From these it's just a hop, skip, and jump to nickname names; after all, they're something we give ourselves all the time now as new online identities.

So it shouldn't be surprising that for the first time since the Age of Aquarius, stylish parents are picking nicknames over their formal versions for their kids, a trend that started with the Brits, whose soap operas are populated by characters with names like Alfie and Edie. But what we're seeing is a whole different genre from the American nickname names of the sixties and seventies—the unisex Cory-Carey-Jodie-Jamie era. The nickname names of today are for the most part short forms of standard appellations, with parents opting for Charlie over Charles and Sam over Samantha.

There are definite pros and cons to using a pet form on the birth certificate. There's no denying their friendly, perky, relaxed yet high-energy appeal, giving a child an air of inviting accessibility, and many of them, like Nellie and Lottie, have a nostalgic, Victorian feel as well. But they are names that never get to grow up, and can be seen as keeping your baby babyish forever. There's a sense of incompleteness, too—your daughter may wonder why she didn't rate a more legitimate name, as may her future employers. But if a hot nickname name is what you're after, here are some of the most appealing:

Girls

ABBY
ADDIE
AGGIE
ALLY
BEA
BILLIE
BIRDIE
CHARLIE
COCO
DAISY
DIXIE
DOLLY
DOT
EDIE
ELLIE
EMMY
EVIE
FANNY
GIGI
GRACIE
HATTIE
IZZY
JOSIE
KATIE
KIKI
KITTY
LETTY
LIBBY
LIL
LO

LOLA
LOTTIE
LOU
LULU
MADDIE/MADDY
MAISIE
MAMIE
MILLIE
MINNIE
MITZI
NELL
NELLIE
NETTIE
NIC
PIPPA
PIXIE
ROSIE
ROXY
SADIE
SAM
TASHA
TAY
TESS
TILLIE
TRIXIE
VIVI
ZUZU

Boys

ACE
ALFIE

ARCHIE	JOE
ARI	LINC
AVI	MAC
BAZ	MISHA
BIX	MOE
BO	MOSE
CAL	NED
CALE	NICO
CHARLIE	OLLIE
CHAZ	OZZIE
CLEM	PACO
DASH	RAFE
DEX	RAY
DEZI	RY
DREW	SASHA
DUKE	SEB
FREDDIE	THEO
GUS	THOM
HARRY	TREY
IKE	VIN
JACE	VING
JACK	WILL
JAX	XAN
JAZZ	ZAK
JEB	ZEB
JED	

Nicknamed Starbabies

ACE	Natalie Appleton, Tom Dumont, Jennie Finch
BEAU	Art Garfunkel, Wendy Wilson, Emma Bunton
BILLIE	Ethan Suplee

BILLY	Helena Bonham Carter & Tim Burton
BIRDIE	Busy Philipps
BUSTER	Michele Hicks & Jonny Lee Miller
CHARLIE	Mimi Rogers, Soledad O'Brien
COCO	Courteney Cox & David Arquette, Diane Farr
DEZI	Jaime Pressly
DIXIE	Tabitha Soren
DUKE	Justine Bateman, Diane Keaton
EDIE	Samantha Morton
EMME	Jennifer Lopez & Marc Anthony
EMMI	Dayna Devon
GENE	Liam Gallagher
GIGI	Cynthia Rowley
GRACIE	Anna Friel & David Thewlis
GUS	Emily Robison
HAPPY	Macy Gray
JACK	Matt Lauer, Luke Perry, and others
JAKE	Tina Yothers
JAX	Gabrielle Beauvais-Nilon
JAZZ	Steffi Graff & Andre Agassi
JOE	Kate Winslet
JOHNNIE (girl)	Melissa Etheridge
JOHNNY	Mira Sorvino
KIT	Jodie Foster
LOLA	Kelly Ripa & Mark Consuelos, Lisa Bonet, Chris Rock, Carnie Wilson
LUCKY	Damon Dash, Cedric the Entertainer
MADDIE	Jamie Lynn Spears
MAGGIE	Jon Stewart
MAX	Christina Aguilera
MILEY	Rev Run

NELL	Helena Bonham Carter & Tim Burton
NICO	Thandie Newton
NIKKO	Brian McKnight
PEANUT	Ingo Rademacher
POPPY	Jamie Oliver
RUDY	Sadie Frost & Jude Law
SADIE	Adam Sandler, Finola Hughes
SAM	Emily Morton, Denise Richards
SASCHA/SASHA	Jessica Sklar & Jerry Seinfeld, Vanessa Williams
SUNNY	Michael Balzary, Adam Sandler
THEO	Cheryl Tiegs
TRIXIE	Damon Wayans
WILL	Wendy Wilson, Meg Tilly & Colin Firth

So Far In They're Out

The whole issue of trendiness and popularity in children's names is a double-sided coin. For the most part, kids are happy having a popular name, equating it with being popular themselves. You won't find many six-year-old Briannas or Bradens out there who say they hate their names. On the other hand, we've all met at least a couple of young adult Jennifers and Joshes who, in retrospect, resent having grown up bearing the epidemic names of the 1970s and '80s. (There have even been support groups for people with the Jennifer Complex.) If you're one of those people, you may well want to choose a name for your baby that's more original than those listed here.

We present the following master list of So Far In They're Out names as a precaution, so that if you do pick one of them for your child, it will be with the knowledge that they embody the trendiness dilemma. Even if there aren't any Sierras or Skylers on your block yet, trust us— they're right around the corner. Some of these represent groups of names that are becoming a little tired from overuse. Western place names, such as Cheyenne and Dakota, no longer sound fresh, and though they are still megapopular, the Hayden/Aidan derivatives—Braden, Brayden, Caden, Kayden, Jaden, Jayden, etc.—have probably reached their peak.

But what if your favorite name is something trendy like Olivia? Either use it anyway, knowing that your Olivia will bring something unique to it, or consider one of substitutes on the list that follows.

SO FAR IN THEY'RE OUT NAMES

Girls
AALIYAH
ALEXA
ALEXANDRIA
ALEXIS
ALLISON
ALYSSA
AMANDA
ASHLEY
ASHLYN/ASHLYNN
AVA
BAILEY
BETHANY
BRIANNA
BRITNEY
BRITTANY
BROOKLYN
DANIELLE
DESTINY
EMILY
EMMA
ESSENCE
HAILEY/HALEY
JADA

JASMINE
JAYLA
JENNA
JENNIFER
JESSICA
JORDAN
KAITLYN
KAYLA
KAYLEE/KAYLEIGH/
  KAYLIE
KELSEY
KYLIE/KYLEE
LAUREN
MacKENZIE/McKENZIE
MADISON
MAKAYLA/MIKAYLA
MARIAH
McKENNA
MEGAN
MORGAN
NEVAEH
OLIVIA
ROSE as a middle name
RYLEE/RYLEIGH

SAMANTHA

SIERRA

SYDNEY

TAYLOR

TRINITY

Boys

ASHTON

AUSTIN

BLAKE

BRADY

BRANDON

BRAYDEN/BRADEN

BRENDAN

CADEN/CAYDEN

CAMERON

CARSON

CARTER

CHANDLER

CODY

DAKOTA

DALTON

DAWSON

DUSTIN

DYLAN

HAYDEN

JAYDEN/JADEN/JAIDEN

JAYLEN

JORDAN

JOSHUA

JUSTIN

KADEN

KYLE

KYLER

LANDON

LOGAN

MASON

MAX

RILEY

RYAN

SEAN

SHANE

SKYLER

TANNER

TAYLOR

TYLER

TYSON

ZACHARY

ZANDER/XANDER

BUT OLIVIA IS MY FAVORITE NAME!

Oh no! Ever since you watched your big sister's copy of *Grease* so many times the tape broke, you've always known that you would name your first daughter Olivia. But now that the time has almost arrived, you find that thousands of other mothers got there first, and Olivia is among the most popular girls' names in the country. What to do?

Well, you have two options. You can stick with your lifelong love despite the perils of superpopularity (three Olivias in each class), or you can look for a worthy substitute, a name that relates to your first choice in style or sound or ethnicity. To help you in the process, here is a list of possible substitutes, all at least a shade more creative and crisp than the well-used original.

Girls

Instead of	Consider
ABIGAIL	ABILENE, ABRA, ANNABEL
ALEXANDRA	ALLEGRA, ALABAMA, TATIANA
ALEXIS	ALBANY, ALICE, ALESSIA
AMANDA	AMABEL, ARAMINTA, MIRANDA
AVA	ADA, AVALON, AVERY
BAILEY	BELLAMY, BAY, BRODY
BRIANNA	BREE, BRYONY, BRONTË
BRITNEY	BRICE, BRYN, BRIGHTON
CHARLOTTE	CLEMENTINE, COLETTE, CELIA
DESTINY	TRUE, DECIMA, DREAM
ELLA	ELLIE, ELLIOT, ELLIS
EMMA	EMMELINE, NORA, EMBETH
GRACE	HONOR, MERCY, VERITY
HAILEY	DAISY, HAVEN, HAZEL
HANNAH	ANYA, DINAH, SANNA
ISABELLA	ARABELLA, MIRABELLA, RAFFAELA
JASMINE	JAMAICA, JACINTA, JAZZ
JAYDEN	JADE, JAY, JANUARY
KAITLYN	BRONWYN, KEIRA, CATE

LAUREN	LAUREL, LAURENZA, MAURA
LILY	LILA, LILAC, IVY
MADISON	MAISIE, MADIGAN, MADRIGAL
MIA	TÉA, MIAMI, MALIA
OLIVIA	OLIVE, OLYMPIA, VALENTINA
RILEY	RHIANNON, RYAN, ROONEY
SAMANTHA	SAMARA, MIRANDA, DIANTHA
SAVANNAH	GEORGIA, ATLANTA, SUSANNAH
SIENNA	RAVENNA, SICILY, CHIARA
SOPHIA	ZOFIA, SOPHIE, STEFANIA

Boys

Instead of	*Consider*
AARON	ABEL, ASA, MICAH
AIDEN	EAMON, DECLAN, FINIAN
ASHTON	ASH, ASPEN, TRENTON
AUSTIN	AUGUST, HOUSTON, AUDEN
BENJAMIN	BENNO, GIDEON, SAMSON
BRADEN	BROCK, CARDEN, WADE
BRODY	BEHAN, BRENNAN, CLOONEY
COOPER	CARVER, CHAPIN, HOPPER
DYLAN	GRIFFIN, BRECCAN, GARETH
ETHAN	EBEN, EZRA, ETIENNE
HAYDEN	HUDSON, SLATER, GRAY
JACKSON	JEFFERSON, TRUMAN, LINCOLN
JACOB	ABEL, JONAS, JUDE
JAKE	MOE, GUS, ELI
JAYDEN	JAGGER, JABEZ, SLADE
JOSHUA	JOSIAH, JUDAH, JETHRO
KYLE	MILES, KALE, KILLIAN
PARKER	BAKER, PAXTON, WHEELER

REED	REEVE, RHYS, EAMES
RYDER	ROMAN, WYLIE, WILDER
TYLER	TOBIAS, THATCHER, TURNER
ZACHARY	ZANE, ZEBEDEE, BARNABY

So Far Out They're In

With names no one ever heard ten years ago catapulting to the top of the popularity list, the adventurous baby namer is forced to bushwack into ever-wilder territory. Some fresh sources for truly original names:

Green Names—Moving beyond Lily and Rose to tree (Beech), water (Bay), and even animal (Pike) names.

Baby Gods & Goddesses—Since we've taken to worshipping our babies, why not name them Jupiter and Juno?

Uncool Names—When you've run out of cool, where do you go? To the Uncool Names, of course, which make Enid and Victor cool again.

The Celts Are Coming—France, Ireland, and Italy are so *done* when it comes to names. What's new: farflung territories like Cornwall (Kerensa), Russia (Dasha), and Tibet (Dainzen).

Unique Names—For those who make sure the url is available before they name the baby, one-of-a-kind names for your little individual.

GREEN NAMES

Being green, as in environmentally conscious, has become not only ethically correct but fashionable. There's a new appreciation for nature in all its glory, and that celebration extends to baby names.

There are several varieties of stylish Green Names that connect with different facets of nature. Most domesticated are the Flower Names, which spring from the sweet Victorian-tinged names popular over the past few decades. Animal names put a more masculine spin on the trend, and water, field, and other nature-word names push the style into wilder territory.

Here, names from this red-hot category:

Flower & Fruit Names

AMANDINE	LAUREL
APPLE	LILAC
ASTER	LILY
AZALEA	LOTUS
BERRY	MAGNOLIA
CAMELLIA	OLIVE
CHERRY	ORCHID
CLOVER	PANSY
DAHLIA	POPPY
DAISY	PLUM
FLEUR	PRIMROSE
FLORA	QUINCE
FREESIA	ROSE
IRIS	VIOLET
IVY	ZINNIA
JONQUIL	

Flower Belle! What a euphonious appellation! Easy on the ears and a banquet for the eyes!

—W. C. Fields, *My Little Chickadee*

Botanical Names

ACACIA

ASH

ASPEN

BANYAN

BEECH

BIRCH

BRANCH

BRIAR

BRYONY

BURR

CEDAR

ELM

FERN

FIELD

FOREST

GROVE

HAZEL

JUNIPER

LAUREL

LEAF

LINDEN

MEADOW

MYRTLE

OAK

PINE

PRAIRIE

SEQUOIA

SPRUCE

WILLOW

Herb & Spice Names

CAYENNE

CINNAMON

CLOVE

FENNEL

HONEY

PEPPER

ROSEMARY

SAFFRON

SAGE

YARROW

Water Names

AQUA

BAY

BEACH

BROOK

FJORD

LAKE

MARSH

NILE

OCEAN/OCEANE/OCEANO

RIO

RIVER

Sky & Weather Names

CLOUD
FROST
RAIN
SKY/SKYE
SNOW
STAR
STORM
SUNNY
SUNSHINE
TEMPEST

Animal & Bird Names

DOVE
DRAKE
FAUNA
FINCH
FOX
HAWK
JAY
LARK
LIONEL
PALOMA
PIKE
RAVEN
ROBIN
TEAL
TROUT
WOLF
WREN

BABY GODS & GODDESSES

You worship your baby, and she's not even born yet! Modern little gods and goddesses are confident and perfect enough to live up to the powerful image of a name like Romeo, Venus, or Adonis. The pantheon of Greek and Roman deities and other classical mythological figures can provide an abundant source of audacious options, all combining deep history with not-heard-in-a-long-time freshness. Here are some of the more interesting choices:

Goddesses

ALALA
ANTHEIA
APHRODITE
ARADIA
ARIADNE
ARTEMIS
ASTRA

ATALANTA

ATHENA

AURORA

BELLONA

CALLIOPE

CERELIA

CERES

CLIO 15

CYBELE

CYNTHIA

DELIA

DEMETER

DIANA

ELARA

ENYO

EOS

FAUNA

FLORA

FORTUNA

GAIA

HERA

IRENE

IRIS

JANA

JUNO

KAMIRA

KORA

LUCINA

LUNA

LYSSA

MAIA

MINERVA

NIKE

PAX

PERSEPHONE

PHOEBE

RHEA

SELENE

THALASSA

THALIA

THEIA

VENUS

VESTA

Gods

ACHILLES

ADONIS

AEOLUS

AGON

AJAX

APOLLO

AQUILO

ARES

ATLAS

AUSTER

CADMUS

CASTOR

COMUS

CRONUS

EROS

HELIOS

HERMES

ICARUS	PARIS
JANUS	PONTUS
JOVE	POSEIDON
JUPITER	SILVANUS
MARS	THANATOS
MERCURY	TRITON
NEPTUNE	VULCAN
ORION	ZEPHYR
PAN	ZEUS

Celestial Starbabies

ATLAS	Anne Heche
AURORA	Nancy McKeon
CALLIOPE	Patricia Arquette (middle name)
CASTOR	James (Metallica) Hetfield
GAIA	Emma Thompson
HERMES	Kelly Rutherford
ICARUS	Lucy Sykes (middle name)
IRENE	Donna Dixon & Dan Ackroyd (middle name)
IRIS	Sadie Frost & Jude Law, Renée O'Connor
LUNA	Frank Lampard
MARS	Sofia Coppola (middle name)
ORION	Chris Noth
PARIS	Pierce Brosnan, Michael Jackson, Rosie O'Donnell
PAX	Angelina Jolie & Brad Pitt
PHOEBE	Bill Gates
ZEPHYR	Karla DeVito & Robby Benson

My husband is pretentious and so am I.

—Gretchen Mol,
explaining her choice of son's name Ptolemy

UNCOOL NAMES

On the heels of such clunky-but-cool hipster favorites as Ruby and Ray come the clunky but, well, *really clunky* names that are so uncool they're cool. You definitely won't be swimming in the mainstream with these assertively unfashionable and some might even say unattractive names. The rationale: Cool has become so pervasive that it just isn't cool anymore.

If you choose one of these names, you better be sure that little Edna is self-confident enough to handle the fallout. Upside: Great-Aunt Edna will be so delighted that you'll find yourself *totally* back in the will.

Girls

AGATHA	FLORENCE
AGNES	FREDERICA
ALBERTA	FREYA
ALMA	FRIEDA
AUGUSTA	GERTRUDE
BERNICE	GLADYS
BEULAH	HARRIET
BLANCHE	HENRIETTA
CONSTANCE	HERMIONE
DRUSILLA	HESTER
EDNA	IDA
ELSIE	JOYCE
ELVIRA	LENORE
ENID	LEONA
ESTELLE	LEONORE
ESTHER	LUCILLE
EUDORA	MILDRED
EUNICE	MINERVA
	MURIEL

MYRA

MYRTLE

NORMA

PENELOPE

PRISCILLA

RUTH

SELMA

THELMA

URSULA

VERA

VIOLA

YVETTE

YVONNE

ZELDA

Boys

ABNER

ALBERT

ALFRED

ARCHIBALD

ARTHUR

BARNEY

BASIL

BERNARD

BORIS

BYRON

CASPER

CHESTER

CLARENCE

CORNELIUS

CYRIL

DIGBY

EDGAR

ELMER

ERNEST

FLOYD

FRANK

FRANKLIN

GILBERT

HARVEY

HERBERT

HIRAM

HOWARD

HUBERT

IRA

JETHRO

JULIUS

LEON

LEOPOLD

LINUS

LLOYD

LOUIS

MARSHALL

MILTON

MORRIS

MURRAY

ORVILLE

OSBERT

OSWALD

OTTO

PERCY	STANLEY
RALPH	VERNON
ROLAND	VICTOR
ROY	VINCENT
SAUL	VIRGIL
SEYMOUR	WALLACE
SIDNEY	WILBUR

THE CELTS ARE COMING

Irish boys' names have ruled fashion for several years now, with Liam and Conor, Ryan and Riley climbing the charts and even crossing over into the girls' territory. Irish surnames such as Delaney and McKenna have been increasingly popular, too.

But now adventurous parents of both girls and boys are exploring the more obscure names of Celtic culture, unusual Irish choices along with undiscovered names from Scotland and Wales, Brittany and Cornwall. It's a rich vein and one that may be of special interest to anyone with family roots in these beautiful corners of the world.

To delve more deeply into Irish name choices, check out our new book, *Cool Irish Names for Babies*.

Girls

AERON—Welsh

AILSA (AYL-sa)—Scottish

AINSLEY (AYNS-lee)—Scottish

AOIFE (EE-feh)—Irish

ARWEN—Welsh

BETHAN—Welsh

BRIONY/BRYONY (BRY-o-nee or BREE-o-nee)—Welsh

BRONWEN—Welsh

CERYS (Ker-is)—Welsh

ELERI—Welsh

ELSPETH—Scottish

ÉMER (EE-mer)—Irish

FIONNUALA (fi-NOO-la)—
   Irish
GWENNO—Welsh
GWYNETH—Welsh
IONA (Eye-OH-na)/IONE
   (Eye-OH-nee)—Scottish
ISHBEL—Scottish
ISLA (EYE-la)—Scottish
JUNO—Irish
KENNA—Scottish
KERENZA—Cornish
LLIO—Welsh
MINIVER—Cornish
NESSA—Scottish
NIAMH (NEEV)—Irish
OLWEN—Welsh
OONA/ÚNA—Irish
RÓISÍN (row-SHEEN)—Irish
RORY—Irish
SAOIRSE (SOR-ka)—Irish
TALULLA—Irish
TAMSIN (TAM-zin)—Cornish
TIERNEY—Irish

Boys
ALASDAIR (AL-us-duhr)—
   Scottish
ANGUS—Scottish
AULAY—Scottish
AURON—Welsh

BASTIAN (BAS-tee-an)—
   Breton
BOWEN—Welsh
BRECON (BREK-on)—Welsh
CALLUM/CALUM—Scottish,
   Irish
CAMBER—Welsh
CIAN/KEAN—Irish
CIARÁN/KIERAN—Irish
CILLIAN/KILLIAN—Irish
CORENTIN(E) (Kor-en-
   TAN)—Breton
CORMAC—Irish
DECLAN—Irish
DENZEL(L)—Cornish
DEVI (DAY-vee)—Breton
DEWI—Welsh
DONNAN—Scottish
DUNCAN—Scottish
EWAN/EWEN (YOO-an)—
   Scottish
FERGUS/FERGUSON—
   Scottish
GARETH—Welsh
GRAHAM/GRAEME—Scottish
GRIFFITH—Welsh
GUTHRIE—Scottish
GWILYM—Welsh
HAMISH (HAY-mish)—Scottish
INNIS (IN-ish)—Scottish

IOLO (YOH-lo)—Welsh

IVAR—Scottish

JAGO (JAHG-O)—Cornish

KEIR (Care)—Scottish

LENNOX—Scottish

MALO (MAH-loh)—Breton

MAXEN—Welsh

MUIR—Scottish

NIALL (NILE)—Scottish

NYE (Nie)—Welsh

OISÍN (O-sheen)—Irish

SEAMUS (SHAY-mus)—Irish

TANGUY/TANGI (TAHN-gee)—Breton

TEILO (TAY-loh)—Welsh

WYN/WYNN—Welsh

UNIQUE—OR CLOSE TO IT—NAMES

When people look for baby names online, they often put in a search for "unique names." Some of them are trying to find names that are unusual and distinctive, but some really do want to give their child a name that's truly one-of-a-kind, something that nobody else has.

One recent newspaper story claimed that one of the reasons for this is because modern parents want their child to be "Googleable," to have a name that's different enough that it will pop online. And some parents say they won't settle on a name until they find out whether its url is available.

Of course, as soon as you give your child a "unique" name, it all but guarantees it won't be unique anymore since someone will almost inevitably poach it. We were tickled to find, for instance, that someone posted on our Web site bulletin board that she'd named her son Knox, a name that wasn't in our or any other baby-naming book—months before Angelina and Brad chose it for their newborn son, launching it on the track to widespread use.

When we asked visitors to our Web site to tell us what they'd named their babies, we never expected their answers to provide such a trove

CALL ME TXT

We've all heard about those Internet-loving parents who named their kids after popular search engines, the @ symbol, and have even replaced Jr. with version 2.0, but if you thought that was weird, check out the new baby-naming trends that have stemmed from the digital age.

It appears young parents are so desperately trying to be techno hip, that they're going so far as to give their offspring names inspired by phonetic spellings typically used in email and text messaging. In a study by McCrindle Research that discusses the Top 10 baby names in Australia, social analyst Mark McCrindle discovered a new naming trend among Generation X.

One of the first things he noticed was that parents were reinventing traditional names like Aidan, Jayden, Kaiden, Amelia, and Brayden by giving them alternate spellings. A further look into the different variations of the names revealed people were adding double letters (Siimon), using hyphens or apostrophes (Emma-Lee), and used phonetic spelling (Jaymz). Phonetic spellers were avidly replacing the *y* with an *i* and the *k* with a *c* in many instances. This resulted in names like Alex-Zander, Aren, Cam'ron, Oskah, Rhyleagh, and Thaillah for the boys and Abbigayle, Ameleiyah, Bre'anna, Emma'lee, Jazmyn, Kaileigh, Krystalle, and Sofiya for girls.   —Yahoo Tech

of highly unusual—yes, even unique—names. Some of these turn gender on its ear, some twist spellings in different ways, some reintroduce ancient or ethnic names or transform place names or surnames, and some are conjured from parents' fertile brains.

Now here is where you would ordinarily expect to find a long list of distinctive, never-heard-before names. But that would be against the spirit of this style. So you'll just have to find—or create—one of your own.

> I want to call our baby Midnight or 411. I really like information, and being a night owl, it's a good fit.
>
> —Will Arnett, whose baby with Amy Poehler was
> ultimately named Archibald

EXTREME EXOTICS

A lot of people have honeymooned in Paris, spent junior year in London, been to Mexico on spring break. But even if you haven't been lucky enough to go to these well-traveled places, at least you've seen them in the movies and on television, learned about their cultures from magazines and language classes.

Hip travel destinations have become ever more exotic, with adventurers pushing into Vietnam and Russia, lolling on the beaches of Syria and climbing the mountains of Tibet. We buy jewelry made in India and clothes worn by Russian supermodels, admire Native American art and read novels set in Afghanistan and Iran. Places and cultures that used to be inaccessible—from once-sleeping giants such as Russia and China to out-of-the-way corners—are now visible and reachable by everyone.

With the world getting smaller in every way, old-school "exotic" names like Danielle and Diego, Sophia and Sean have lost a good measure of their intrigue. Parents in search of an international option these days need to look farther afield, to such previously uncharted baby-naming territories as Asia and the Middle East, Eastern Europe and the South Seas.

Here, a selection of names from far-flung locales. For more ideas, see the lists of African names on page 177, of unusual international options on page 191, the Celtic names on page 49, and on nameberry.com.

Girls

ADARA—Arabic
AIKO—Japanese
AILANI—Hawaiian
AJEYA—Hindi
AMIRA—Arabic
ANAHITA—Iranian
ANNUSHKA—Russian
AOLANI—Hawaiian
ARANTXA (ah-RAHN-cha)—
  Basque
ASHA—Hindi
AYAKO—Japanese
AZA—Arabic
AZAMI—Japanese
AZIZAH—Arabic
BAHAAR—Hindi
BAI—Chinese
BEEJA—Hindi
CHARU—Hindi
CYRA—Iranian
DARYA—Russian
DHARA—Hindi
DEVI—Hindi

FEODORA—Russian
GEN—Japanese
IMAKO—Japanese
IRINA—Russian, Eastern
  European
JAMILA—Hindi
JUN—Japanese
KALA—Hindi
KALILA—Arabic
KALOLA—Hawaiian
KAZUKO—Japanese
KIMANA—Native American
KIRI—Maori
LALA—Hawaiian
LALEH—Iranian
LEOLANI—Hawaiian
LILIYA—Russian, Ukrainian
LUDMILA—Slavic
MIN—Chinese
MONSERRAT—Catalan
NIABI—Native American
NILEY—Aboriginal
PARVANA—Iranian
RASHIDA—Hindi

REZ—Hungarian
SAHAR—Arabic, Iranian
SANJANA—Hindi
SAVITA—Hindi
SUKI—Japanese
TENZIN—Tibetan
ZOSIA—Polish
ZUZELA—Native American

Boys
AARU—Egyptian
AKIO—Japanese
ALEXEI—Russian
ANATOLY—Russian
ARJUN—Hindi
ARKADI—Russian
BARDO—Aboriginal
BHANU—Hindi
CASIMIR—Polish
DAINZIN—Tibetan
DEVEN—Hindi
DMITRI—Russian
EIJI (EE-jee)—Japanese
FYODOR—Russian
HIROSHI—Japanese
INIGO—Basque
JAHAN—Hindi
JIRO—Japanese
JIVAN—Hindi
KADIR—Hindi

KENJI—Japanese
KEO—Hawaiian
KHALIL—Arabic, Hindi
KOJI—Japanese
LEV—Russian
LUKA—Hawaiian
OSMAN—Turkish
OZURU—Japanese
PAAVO—Finnish
PATRIN—Gypsy
RAFIQ—Hindi
REWI—Maori
RODION—Russian
SAJAN—Hindi
SANDOR (SHAN-dor)—
  Hungarian
SERGEI—Russian
SHIRO—Japanese
SIVAN—Kurdish
TAMATI—Maori
TARIQ—Arabic
TIBOR—Slavic
TOMEK—Polish
VADIM—Russian
WIT (Veet)—Polish
YUKIO—Japanese
ZIVEN—Slavic
ZOLTAN—Hungarian
ZUBIN—Persian, Hebrew

OFF THE MAP

While some of us are traveling perhaps a bit less than we used to, we can still reminisce about the places we've seen—maybe the balmy beach where we honeymooned—or dream about delicious destinations we've yet to experience—the hill towns of Tuscany, the tropical West Indies. Beautiful places with beautiful names: some of them beautiful enough to bestow on our babies. If they have personal significance for you, so much the better.

Here's an around-the-world guide to some of the more untouristed place names:

ABILENE	DONEGAL
AJA	DUBLIN
ALVARADO	GENOA
AMALFI	GUERNSEY
ANDORRA	IBIZA
AREZZO	INYO
BAHAMA	JAVA
BOLIVIA	KEA
BRAY	LARAMIE
CABO	LAREDO
CADIZ	LEANDRO
CAIRO	LEITH
CALAIS	LILLE
CALEDONIA	MACON
CALGARY	MADEIRA
CARRARA	MAILI
CAYMAN	MAJORCA
DIJON	MALMÖ

MALTA	SALEM
MARBELLA	SAMOA
MESA	SEQUOIA
MIAMI	SICILY
MILAN	SOLANA
MISSOULA	SWANSEA
NAVARRE	TAHOE
NAZAIRE	TRINIDAD
NEVADA	TULSA
OCALA	VALENCIA
ODESSA	VENICE/VENEZIA
PARMA	VERONA
PERU	VIENNA
PIRAEUS	VIOTA
QUEBEC	ZAMORA
QUITO	ZHODA
RIO	ZUMA

Image

Want a name that underscores your own Hip Mama or Cool Daddy image? In this section we look at Hipster Names and Yupster Names, help you figure out the difference, and offer a selection that will fit right in with your vintage diaper bag and Bugaboo stroller.

If getting your child into Harvard is more important to you than hipster cred, we look at which traditional, grown-up names sound serious, with extra credit for Presidential Names. Or if you prefer to nurture a little artist, we offer the Creative Names, choices inspired by authors, painters, designers, musicians, and their creations.

Unusual names are certainly stylish, but how will having one affect your child? We examine that issue, along with the impact of nicknames and the delicate question of class and names.

And finally, if you're looking for a name that offers the perfect balance between popular and unique, between fitting in and standing out, we offer that very special selection, too.

Hipster Names

The hipster parent is a relatively new being, arriving with the wave of young rock- and film-star moms and pops out to prove that city life, tattoos, and skinny hips can coexist with strollers and diapers.

Along with a black Bugaboo and a onesie reading "Frankly, my parents are not fit for this," a hipster baby needs a hipster name. While hipster names are partly a matter of style—and we considered putting this chapter in the Style section—they're more, we think, an issue of image. Hipster names are not necessarily new or fashionable in any conventional sense, but more likely to be quirky and cool in an understated way. A nonhipster may have a difficult time identifying a hipster name as one that has any kind of style value, while another hipster will recognize it immediately as hip.

Hipsters have a horror of conformity—once a former hipster name like Ava, for instance, gets too popular, they abandon it—they're also unlikely to stray far from their own pack. Why? Because the only thing a hipster hates more than being seen as a hipster is *not* being seen as a hipster.

And then, of course, there are the wannabe hipsters who don't know that Oscar has been done to death, and the avant-garde hipsters who would rather wear Liz Claiborne and drive a Nissan Sentra than give a baby any name that was even vaguely likely to land on this list.

Here, the hipster names most often heard around Brooklyn and Santa Monica, Austin and Madison these days (though we can't resist pointing out that the *names* Brooklyn, Monica, Austin, and Madison are nowhere among them):

Girls

ANNABEL	LULU
ANTONIA	LUNA
BILLIE	MAEVE
CLEMENTINE	MAMIE
DAISY	MATILDA
DELILAH	MAUDE
DIXIE	MAY
EDITH	MILLIE
ELLA	MINNIE
FLORA	NATASHA
FRANCES	NELL
GEORGIA	OLIVE
HAZEL	OPAL
INDIA	PALOMA
IONE/IONA	PEARL
IRIS	PHOEBE
ISLA	PIPER
IVY	PIPPA
JULIET	POLLY
JUNE	POPPY
LENA	ROMY
LILA	RUBY
LUCIA	SADIE
	SCARLETT

SOPHIE

STELLA

TALULLAH

TILLIE

WILLA

VIOLET

Boys

ACE

ARTHUR

ASHER

ATTICUS

AUGUST

AUGUSTIN

BUTCH

DASHIELL

DEX/DEXTER

DONOVAN

DUKE

ELVIS

FELIX

FINN

FRANK

GUS

HARRY

HARVEY

HOMER

HUDSON

HUGO

IGNATIUS

IKE

INIGO

ISAAC

ISAIAH

JACKSON

KINGSTON

LEOPOLD

LEVI

MAGNUS

MILES

MILO

MOSES

ORSON

OSCAR

OTIS

OTTO

QUENTIN

QUINCY

PENN

PHINEAS

REUBEN

ROMAN

ROSCOE

RUFUS

RUPERT

SEBASTIAN

SILAS

THADDEUS

THEO

WYATT

ZAN/ZANDER

Either

HARPER	RILEY
HOPPER	ROWAN
JAGGER	SAWYER
KAI	SULLIVAN
LENNON	TRUE
LUCA	WEST
RAY	ZION

Yupster Names

What's the difference between a yupster and a hipster? Well, a yupster is more likely to be suburban, while a hipster is urban—in sensibility if not in fact. A yupster is more frankly middle-class, more bourgeois, more mainstream. A yupster may be a former hipster who's crossed over to a more conventional adult life: bought a house in Montclair or Evanston, given up the dream of becoming a rock star or a screen-writer and taken a job in marketing.

Yupster names are more traditional than hipster names, too: perhaps further up the popularity ladder, or more conventional in other ways. Olive is hipster, Olivia is yupster; Hugo is hipster, Henry is yupster. Is there any crossover? A bit, though less than you might think. The less ordinary yupster names—Alice, Eliza, and Emmett, for instance—might be used by bona fide hipsters, while hipster names that get popular may become fit for yupster consumption.

The yupster names most prevalent today include:

Girls	CAROLINE
ALICE	CHARLOTTE
AMELIA	CHLOE
ANNA	CLAIRE

ELEANOR	COLIN
ELIZA	CONOR
ELIZABETH	EMMETT
EMMA	ETHAN
GRACE	EVAN
HOPE	HENRY
ISABEL	JACK
JULIA	JACKSON
KATE	JAMES
LAURA	JONAH
LILY	JULIAN
LUCY	JUSTIN
MADELEINE	LEO
MIA	LIAM
MIRANDA	LUCAS
MOLLY	LUKE
NATALIE	MAX
OLIVIA	NATHAN
ROSE	NATHANIEL
SARAH	NICHOLAS
SOPHIA	NOAH
SYDNEY	OLIVER
TESS/TESSA	OWEN
ZOE	SAM
	SPENCER
Boys	TOBIAS
ALEXANDER	WILL
CHARLES	

Unusual Names

More and more children are getting unusual or even unique—as in one-of-a-kind names—and fewer and fewer are given the most popular names than ever before. To fill the gap, there is an ever-expanding supply of unusual names out there for parents to choose from: international names from all over the world and word names and surname names and place names that weren't commonly used as first names or flat out didn't exist before.

Why the shift? In our increasingly standardized society—the same stores in every mall in every town, the same brands in every store—more parents want a name that will make their children stand out. And since we've become more aware of the capacity of branding, we're also more aware of the capacity of a name to create a distinctive identity. Celebrity culture is influential as well, with stars both having unusual names—from Beyoncé to Leighton—and choosing them for their children: as in Tennyson and Suri, not to mention Moxie Crime-Fighter and Bronx Mowgli.

The big question is, will having an unusual name help or hurt your child?

Old academic studies that linked unusual names with poor school performance and "psychoneurosis" are no longer relevant in this new era, when having a name that's different from everybody else's has become, well, the norm. And if you're worried about playground teasing, that is happening less and less—after all, what ammunition can Ptolemy come up with to taunt Titan or Tulip? So you don't have to fear the unknown or uncommon—as long as you keep your choice within the realm of reason.

There are thousands of unusual names to choose from in our books *The Baby Name Bible* and *Cool Names for Babies* and on our Web site, nameberry.com, ranging from the slightly quirky to the truly obscure. You'll find lots of unconventional choices in other sections of this book, too, but here's a compendium of some of the best of the most usable unusuals.

Girls

ABIJAH	FENELLA
ANDROMEDA	GALEN
ANEMONE	GENOA
AQUE	IANTHE
ARAMINTA	ILARIA
ATLANTA	ILESHA
BAYO	INDRE
CERES	JACARANDA
CORISANDE	JAVA
CRESSIDA	JETHRA
DESDEMONA	JONQUIL
DEVI	KAMARIA
DHARMA	KELILA
DIA	KERENSA
DRUSILLA	LETHA
ELIORA	LINDEN
ELUNED	LORCA
ENGRACIA	MAB
	MELANTHA

NOOR	AZARIAH
OONA	BADER
OUIDA	BAZ
OZARA	BEACON
PALLAS	BIX
PANDORA	BOAZ
PAZIAH	CALIXTO
PERSEPHONE	CHAUCER
PHAEDRA	CHEEVER
POLEXIA	CHRISTO
QUELLA	CREW
RAZIELLA	EMO
REZ	HAROUN
SABRA	HORACIO
SAHAR	IZAN
SEDONA	KALMAN
SURYA	KEES
TANAQUIL	KELSO
TEMPLE	MARS
TRILBY	NAPIER
VELVET	NEO
VENEZIA	NEPTUNE
XANTHO	QUITO
XIA	ROGAN
ZAMORA	ZENO
ZARIZA	ZINC

Boys

	Either
AKIM	ALDEN
AMIAS	ARA
AXTON	BIRD

BRAZIL	KEIL
BRIO	KEW
BURNE	LUNDY
CARBRY	MACON
CARDEN	OBERON
CURRAN	ROMNEY
DAY	UMBER
DESTRY	UTAH
EZRI	VAIL
GILBY	VEGA
GOLDEN	WAVERLY
HOLLAND	ZEPHYR
JOURNEY	

And just to show that we're not making all this up, the following is a list of actual names that were given to babies born in Georgia between 1990 and 2007, according to ajc.com, the Web site of the *Atlanta Journal-Constitution,* the state's largest newspaper. For the full list, go to http://projects.ajc.com/names/list/.

ACCORD	BOSNIA
ALGERIA	BUTTERFLY
ARAXA	CAMBRIDGE
ARUBA	CELEBRITY
ATTORNEY	CIVIC
AURA	COBRA
AXIOM	COYOTE
BADGER	DIJON
BEIGE	DRESDEN
BETHLEHEM	EDGE
BOISE	ERMINE

ESPRIT	PLATINUM
FALL	QUANTUM
GEO	QUEBEC
HEAVEN-LEIGH	QUEEN-ISIS
JAGUAR	RAIDER
KIWI	SAFARI
KODIAK	SOLDIER
LATVIA	SWAN
LEBANON	TUNDRA
LEGEND	UNO
LYNX	VIPER
MALLARD	VISION
MARRIOTT	WISTERIA
MYSTIQUE	WRANGLER
NEON	XA
PEACOCK	XIAN
PIKE	ZIMBABWE

Everyone I know with an unusual name loves it. It's only the losers named Dave that think having an unusual name is bad, and who cares what they think. They're named Dave.

   —Penn Jillette, father of Moxie CrimeFighter and Zolten

But Seriously . . .

If you're feeling sick of ever-changing fads and fashions, names that scamper up and down the popularity lists, and are tired of the rampant striving for "creativity" and "uniqueness," the names listed below come with a lifetime warranty; they are built to last from babyhood to modern maturity. Solid, enduring, no-nonsense, no-frills classics with real history, they substitute substance for trendiness, impressive for cute. To prospective interviewers for Ivy League colleges and for prominent positions down the road, they project an image of professionalism and competence. Of course, if you find some of them too solemn and serious in the meantime, many of them come with livelier nicknames: no reason why baby Josephine can't be called Josie or little Abraham be known as Baby Abie. So here is a list of honest, straightforward, grown-up baby names:

Girls

ABIGAIL

ADA

AGATHA

AGNES

ALBERTA

ALICE

ANN

ANNA

AUGUSTA

BEATRICE

CAROLINE

CATHERINE	JOANNA
CHARLOTTE	JOSEPHINE
CLAIRE	JUDITH
CLARA	JULIA
CONSTANCE	KATE
CORA	KATHERINE
CORNELIA	KAY
DORA	LAURA
DOROTHY	LOUISE
EDITH	MARGARET
EDNA	MARIAN
ELEANOR	MARTHA
ENID	MARY
ESTHER	MATILDA
EUDORA	MAUDE
EVELYN	MIRIAM
FAITH	NAOMI
FLORA	NORA
FLORENCE	OLIVE
FRANCES	PAULA
GRACE	PAULINE
HARRIET	PATIENCE
HAZEL	PENELOPE
HELEN	PRISCILLA
HONOR	PRUDENCE
HOPE	ROSALIND
IDA	RUTH
IRENE	SYLVIA
IRIS	THELMA
JANE	URSULA
JEAN	VIRGINIA

VIVIAN

WINIFRED

Boys

ABRAHAM

ALBERT

ALFRED

ARTHUR

BENEDICT

CARL

CHARLES

CLARENCE

CLAUDE

CLIVE

CONRAD

CYRUS

EDMUND

EDWARD

ELLIOT

EPHRAIM

ERNEST

EUGENE

EUSTACE

EVERETT

FRANCIS

FREDERICK

GEORGE

HORACE

HORATIO

HUGH

JOHN

JOSIAH

LAWRENCE

LEMUEL

LEON

LEONARD

LEWIS

LINCOLN

LLOYD

LUTHER

MARTIN

MOSES

NATHANIEL

OGDEN

PAUL

PHILIP

RALPH

REED

ROGER

SILAS

THEODORE

VICTOR

WALTER

WESTON

WILSON

WOODROW

PRESIDENTIAL POWER

The election of Barack Obama has inspired an unprecedented number of baby Baracks, Obamas, and even Michelles, Malias, and Sashas. Former presidents' names are also options, for what could be more serious, imposing, and distinguished than a Chief Executive name? Here are some presidential picks that could give your little boy (or—why not?—girl) some instant gravitas.

ABRAHAM	MADISON
CALVIN	McKINLEY
CARTER	MONROE
CHESTER	PIERCE
CLEVELAND	QUINCY
CLINTON	REAGAN
DELANO	TAFT
GARFIELD	TAYLOR
GRANT	THEODORE
GROVER	TRUMAN
HARRISON	TYLER
HAYES	ULYSSES
JACKSON	WILSON
JEFFERSON	WOODROW
KENNEDY	ZACHARY
LINCOLN	

—And a few First Ladies (and Daughters) as well:

ABIGAIL	DOLLEY
CHELSEA	ELEANOR
CLAUDIA	ELIZA

GRACE	LOU
HILLARY	LOUISA
JACQUELINE	LUCRETIA
JENNA	MALIA
JULIA	MAMIE
LAURA	MICHELLE
LETITIA	SASHA

In those old days, the average man called his children after his most revered and historical idols; consequently there was hardly a family, at least in the West, but had a Washington in it—and also a Lafayette, a Franklin, and six or eight sounding names from Byron, Scott, and the Bible, if the offspring held out.

—Mark Twain, *The Gilded Age*

Creative Names

Maybe you're a creative person, an artist of some kind, or simply someone who prizes inventiveness and originality. And you want your child's name to convey a creative image, too, to suggest someone who's a dancer or a painter, the kind of person who's great with color and can spin songs from the air and who puts their own distinctive stamp on everything they do.

You might get by now that there's a subtle difference between names that carry a creative image and those that are creative in themselves. Examples: Kal-El might be a creative name, but Kalindi conveys a more creative image. Shepherd is a creative name, but Seraphina has a more creative image.

And it's image we're concerned with here. How do you find a name that carries a creative image?

There are a couple of different avenues. One is to draw from the actual names of creative people: writers, musicians, artists, dancers. You can either just choose a name you like from this group, or choose the name because you love the work of the artist who made it famous, as Brad Pitt did when he named his daughter after architect Nouvel or Woody Allen did when he named his daughter Bechet after one of his favorite jazz-musician heroes.

Please note, though, that not every creative genius's name has a creative aura: You may adore Jane Austen or John Cheever, but the name Jane or John is not going to get anyone's creative blood racing.

Some of the best choices in this class:

ART

Girls	Boys
DELAUNAY	AMEDEO
FRIDA	ANGELICO
GEORGIA	ANSEL
GOYA	ANSELM
IMOGEN	CALDER
INDIANA	CHRISTO
KARA	CLAES
KIKI	CORNELL
MAGRITTE	COROT
MANET	CY
MARIN	DIX
MARISOL	GRECO
MATTA	HOPPER
MONET	JACKSON
NAN	JASPER
PICABIA	JUDD
ROBBIA	KEES
SERRA	LEONARDO
SOUTINE	MIRÓ
VIEIRA	MOORE
	PABLO

PENN
PICASSO
PIET
RAPHAEL
RODIN
SARGENT
TURNER
WESTON
WILLEM
WINSLOW

Either
BASQUIAT
BLAKE
BRAQUE
CURRAN

DUFY
GAUGUIN
HARTIGAN
KAHLO
KLEE
MANZU
MARDEN
MIRÓ
NEO
O'KEEFFE
REM
REMINGTON
RODIN
ROUSSEAU
WYETH

FASHION & DESIGN

Girls
AGYNESS
ALAIA
BALENCIAGA
CHANEL
COCO
DARYA
DIOR
DONATELLA
DOUTZEN

ELLE
FREJA
GISELE
GUCCI
KAMALI
KASIA
KINGA
KRIZIA
L'WREN
LIYA

MALGOSIA	MANOLO
MIUCCIA	MIES
PALOMA	NARCISO
PICABIA	VALENTINO
PRADA	VENTURI
SHALOM	YVES
SIRI	
STELLA	**Either**
SUVI	AALTO
TYRA	ARMANI
VIEIRA	DIOR
VIVIENNE	EAMES
ZANDRA	GEHRY
	ISSEY
Boys	JOURDAN
CONRAN	LOEWY
DRIES	MORI
EERO	NOUVEL
FABIEN	PEI
FORD	PELLI
GERRIT	PIANO
HARDY	PONTI
HERMÉS	REM
INIGO	SHAHN
JENSEN	VENTURI
KENZO	VIONNET

LITERATURE

Girls
ANAÏS
ANGELOU
APHRA
AYN
BRONTË
COLETTE
DJUNA
EDITH
EUDORA
FLANNERY
JESSAMYN
MAYA
PLUM
RUMER
SONNET
THISBE
WILLA
ZADIE
ZOLA
ZORA

Boys
BALDWIN
BECKETT
BYRON
CAIN
CONRAD
COOPER

DAMON
DANTE
DASHIELL
EZRA
HAMMETT
HOMER
HUGO
ISHMAEL
KEATS
MORRISON
PLATO
ROALD
RUNYON
SVEVO
TRUMAN
ZANE

Either
ALCOTT
AMIS
AUDEN
AUGUST
AUSTEN
AUSTER
BALLARD
BEHAN
BELLOW
BENÉT
BLAKE

BLY	LAFCADIO
BYATT	LANGSTON
CAIN	LARDNER
CARSON	LE CARRÉ
CARVER	LIONEL
CHANDLER	LONDON
CHEEVER	LORCA
COOPER	LOWELL
CRANE	MALLARMÉ
DIDION	McEWAN
DYLAN	MEHTA
ELIOT	MILAN
ELLISON	MILLAY
EMERSON	MOSS
FITZGERALD	MUNRO
FORSTER	NERUDA
FROST	O'CASEY
GALWAY	PAZ
GIDE	POE
GLASGOW	RALEIGH
HARPER	RHYS
HART	RING
HARTE	SALINGER
HEMINGWAY	SAROYAN
JARRELL	SHAW
JERZY	TENNESSEE
JUNOT	TENNYSON
KEATS	THACKERAY
KEROUAC	THEROUX
KESEY	THOREAU

THURBER
TWAIN
VIDAL

WALKER
YEATS

MUSIC & DANCE

Girls
AALIYAH
ABBA
ALANIS
ARETHA
ASHANTI
BEYONCÉ
BILLIE
BLU
CHAKA
DINAH
EARTHA
ELLA
ENYA
ETTA
GELSEY
HOLIDAY
ISADORA
LATIFAH
MACY
MADONNA
MAHALIA
MARIAH

MARLEY
MYA
NIRVANA
ODETTA
PIAF
RIHANNA
SADE
SANTANA
SHAKIRA
SHANIA
TANAQUIL
TWYLA

Boys
AMADEUS
ARLO
ARMSTRONG
AXL
BING
BIX
BONO
CALE
CARUSO

COLEMAN	**Either**
COLTRANE	BAEZ
DION	BASIE
DJANGO (the *D* is	BECHET
silent)	BECK
ELTON	BOWIE
ELVIS	BRAHMS
FABIAN	CAB
GARTH	CALE
GERSHWIN	CALLAS
HENDRIX	CALLOWAY
JARRETT	CROSBY
KANYE	DENVER
KENTON	DONOVAN
LOUDON	DUFF
MILES	DYLAN
MISHA	ELLINGTON
MORRISON	EVERLY
MOZART	GILLESPIE
OTIS	GUTHRIE
PLACIDO	JAGGER
PRINCE	JOPLIN
RUFUS	JOSS
THELONIOUS	KELIS
USHER	LENNON
WOLFGANG	LENNOX
WYCLEF	LIONEL
WYNTON	MINGUS
ZEVON	PRESLEY
ZUBIN	QUINCY

RAMONE   VERDI
RAY

Another approach is to use words associated with some branch of the arts as names: Cadence, for instance, or Sonnet. Here are some possibilities:

Girls
ALLEGRA
ARIA
CADENCE
CALLIOPE
CALYPSO
CYMBELINE
FIFE
JAZ(Z)
LYRIC
PIPER
POET
SONNET
VIOLA

Boys
ALTO

BANJO
BRIO
CELLO
CLAY
PENN
REBOP
SAX

Either
BELL
DRUM
HARPER
MUSIC
PAINTER
QUILL
SAYER
STORY

CREATIVO

And then there is a group of names that sound creative not because of any association with a creative person or thing, but simply because they project an artistic image and feel. Of course, as the boundaries of baby naming push ever outward, this group keeps growing. Many of the more exotic international names might be considered creative, along with word names and nature names and unusual old names and invented names. You'll find thousands more throughout this book and on nameberry.com. Here's a selection of the best:

Girls

ABRA
ALLEGRA
ARABELLA
ARIADNE
ARIEL
ASTRA
AURORA
CANDIDA
CASSANDRA
CLEA
CLEO/CLIO
DORIAN
ELECTRA
ESMÉ
EVANGELINE
FLEUR
GABRIELLA
GABRIELLE
GENEVA
INDIA
IONE
ISOLDE
JESSAMINE
KAIA
KEZIAH
KYRA
LETA
LILIANA
LILICA
LUNA
MARA
MIRABEL
NADIA
NATALYA
NEVE
NICOLA
ODETTE
ORIANA
PANDORA
PETRA
PILAR
PORTIA
QUINTANA
QUINTINA
RAFFAELA
ROMY
SHOSHANA

SIMONE
SONYA
TALIA
TALULLAH
TAMARA
TATIANA
THEA
VALENTINA
ZAHARA
ZANDRA

Boys
AMEDEO
AMYAS
BARNABY
BENNO
BOAZ
CORRADO
DMITRI
ELLERY
ENZO
EPHRAIM
FLORIAN
GRAY
GULLIVER
JASPER
JETHRO
JOSIAH
LORENZO
LUCIAN
MARCO

MICAH
MISHA
MOSES
ORLANDO
ORSON
PHILO
PHINEAS
QUENTIN
RAOUL
ROLLO
SOREN
TAJ
TARQUIN
THADDEUS
THEO
TRISTAN
ZEPHYR

Either
BAY
CERULEAN
DOON/DUNE
EMERY
INDIGO
NICO
NORTH
ORION
RIO
SASHA
XAN
ZEN

FICTIONAL CHARACTERS

Names of characters on television, in movies, and in books can influence the names of real-life babies. Witness Addison, the *Grey's Anatomy* name that's the new Madison AND the new Allison. Or Trinity, the name from *The Matrix* that inspired thousands of little namesakes.

What follows are the most influential character names, most of them from newer and better-known sources. For an even more comprehensive list, please see *Cool Names for Babies*.

Movies

AMÉLIE	*Amélie*
ARWEN	*Lord of the Rings*
ASPEN	*Bedtime Stories*
BARDOLPH	*Cold Mountain*
BELLA	*Twilight*
BROM	*Eragon*
CHASE (f)	*Batman Forever*
CLARICE	*Silence of the Lambs*
DOMINO (f)	*Domino*
DRAVEN	*In the Shadows*
ELLE	*Legally Blonde*
EVEY	*V for Vendetta*
FLINT	*Spider-Man 3*
GRIET (f)	*Girl with a Pearl Earring*
GRAY (f)	*Catch & Release*
JUBA (m)	*Gladiator*
JUNO	*Juno*
KALE (m)	*Disturbia*
KLAATU (m)	*The Day the Earth Stood Still*
LATIKA	*Slumdog Millionaire*

LUCIUS	*The Dark Knight*
LUX (f)	*The Virgin Suicides*
MAXIMUS	*Gladiator*
MIDNIGHT (m)	*Constantine*
MIRANDA	*The Devil Wears Prada*
NAPOLEON	*Napoleon Dynamite*
NEO (m)	*The Matrix*
NOLA	*Match Point*
OLIVE	*Little Miss Sunshine*
OLYMPIAS	*Alexander*
PADMÉ	*Star Wars: Revenge of the Sith*
POLEXIA	*Almost Famous*
POPPY	*Happy-Go-Lucky*
PTOLEMY	*Alexander*
ROUX (m)	*Chocolat*
SATINE	*Moulin Rouge*
SHEBA	*Notes on a Scandal*
SILK	*Watchmen*
STRAWBERRY	*Quantum of Solace*
TRINITY	*The Matrix*
TRIP	*The Virgin Suicides*
TUGG	*Tropic Thunder*
ULYSSES	*O Brother, Where Art Thou?*
VESPER (f)	*Casino Royale*

Television

ADDISON (f)	*Grey's Anatomy*
ADRIAN	*Monk*
ARI	*Entourage*
ASTER	*Dexter*
AUDI (f)	*Dexter*

BLAIR (f)	*Gossip Girl*
BREE	*Desperate Housewives*
CALLIE	*Grey's Anatomy*
CATALINA	*My Name Is Earl*
CELIA	*Weeds*
CREED	*The Office*
CRICKET	*The Starter Wife*
DEXTER	*Dexter*
DIXON	*90210*
EDIE	*Desperate Housewives*
GABRIELLE	*Desperate Housewives*
GAIUS	*Battlestar Galactica*
GEORDI	*Star Trek: The Next Generation*
HANK	*Californication*
HIRO	*Heroes*
HORATIO	*CSI: Miami*
IGNACIO	*Ugly Betty*
ISAAC	*Heroes*
ISOBEL/IZZIE	*Grey's Anatomy*
JACK	*24, 30 Rock*
JUDAH	*Weeds*
KIMA	*The Wire*
KITTY	*Brothers & Sisters*
LAFAYETTE	*True Blood*
LAVENDER	*The Starter Wife*
LENNOX	*24*
MICAH	*Heroes*
MIRANDA	*Grey's Anatomy*
NATE	*Gossip Girl*
NICOLETTE	*Big Love*
ORSON	*Desperate Housewives*

PRESTON	*Grey's Anatomy*
ROMAN	*Big Love*
RUFUS	*Gossip Girl*
SERENA	*Gossip Girl*
SILAS	*Weeds*
SOOKIE	*True Blood*
TANCY	*Big Love*
TRIPP (nickname)	*Dirty Sexy Money*
VICTORY	*Lipstick Jungle*
WILHELMINA	*Ugly Betty*
ZIVA	*NCIS*

MAD MEN NAMES

The hep, keen TV show *Mad Men*, set in JFK-era New York, gets all the period details right, including the names. Are parents ready to adopt the show's now-quaint monikers? Maybe not quite yet, but don't be surprised if you have grandchildren named Don and Betty.

BERTRAM	MIDGE
BETTY	PAUL
DON	PEGGY
FRANCINE	PETE
FREDDY	RACHEL
HARRY	ROGER
HELEN	SALVATORE
JOAN	TRUDY
KEN	

"Olivia" and "Elliot" sound less like tough cops than febrile poets or drawing-room-comedy characters. It's as if these softer, kinder sounds were secret selves and dream identities.

On naming the characters in *Law & Order: Special Victims Unit*
—John Leonard, *New York*

Books

ABELARD	*The Brief Wondrous Life of Oscar Wao*
ALHAMBRA	*The Accidental*
ALMA	*The History of Love*
AURELIUS (f)	*The Thirteenth Tale*
BELLA	The Twilight Saga
BENNINGTON (f)	*Going Down*
BLUE (f)	*Special Topics in Calamity Physics*
BRIONY	*Atonement*
CALLIOPE	*Middlesex*
CASSIE	*In the Woods, The Likeness*
DAWSEY (m)	*The Guernsey Literary and Potato Peel Pie Society*
EDGAR	*The Story of Edgar Sawtelle*
ELLIS (f)	*And Now You Can Go*
FALMOUTH (m)	*You Don't Love Me Yet*
FAUNIA	*The Human Stain*
FEATHER	*Bad Boy Brawly Brown*
FIG (f)	*The Man of My Dreams*
HIERONYMOUS/ HARRY	*City of Bones*
KIKI	*On Beauty*
KINSEY (f)	Sue Grafton's alphabet mysteries
MAGNUS	*The Accidental*
MARISOL	*The Brief Wondrous Life of Oscar Wao*
MINGUS	*The Fortress of Solitude*

MISHA (m)	*Absurdistan*
OSCAR	*The Brief Wondrous Life of Oscar Wao*
OSKAR	*Extremely Loud and Incredibly Close*
PRECIOUS	*The No. 1 Ladies' Detective Agency*
SAI (f)	*The Inheritance of Loss*
SAMSON	*Man Walks into a Room*
TOWNER (f)	*The Lace Reader*
VALENTINO	*What Is the What*
VIDA	*The Thirteenth Tale*
ZORA	*On Beauty*

LASTING LITERARY CHARACTER NAMES

The pages of literature are filled with characters whose names are both common and uncommon (some completely invented by the author), ephemeral and enduring. Some have left a permanently negative impression—Ebenezer was forever Scrooged by Dickens, as was Uriah (Heep), and most people would want to stay away from Iago and Draco and Queeg. But there are many more admirable examples of memorable characters with memorable names, including:

ABRA	*East of Eden*
ATTICUS	*To Kill a Mockingbird*
BRETT (f)	*The Sun Also Rises*
CHANCE (Chauncey)	*Being There*
CLARISSA	*Mrs. Dalloway*
DAISY	*Daisy Miller, The Great Gatsby*
DARCY	*Pride and Prejudice*

(continued)

DOMINIQUE	*The Fountainhead*
DORIAN	*The Picture of Dorian Gray*
EMMA	*Emma, Madame Bovary*
ESMÉ	*For Esmé, With Love and Squalor*
ESTELLA	*Great Expectations*
FLEUR	*The Forsyte Saga*
GUINEVERE	*Knights of the Round Table*
HEATHCLIFF	*Wuthering Heights*
HERMIONE	Harry Potter books
HOLDEN	*The Catcher in the Rye*
ISADORA	*Fear of Flying*
JUDE	*Jude the Obscure*
LOLITA	*Lolita*
MARIN	*A Book of Common Prayer*
MILO	*Catch-22*
NATASHA	*War and Peace*
NORA	*A Doll's House*
OPHELIA	*Hamlet*
PEARL	*The Scarlet Letter*
PILAR	*For Whom the Bell Tolls*
PORTIA	*The Merchant of Venice*
REGAN	*King Lear*
RHETT	*Gone with the Wind*
SABRA	*Cimarron*
SCARLETT	*Gone with the Wind*
SCOUT	*To Kill a Mockingbird*
SEBASTIAN	*Brideshead Revisited*
SIDDA	*Divine Secrets of the Ya-Ya Sisterhood*
VELVET	*National Velvet*
ZOOEY	*Franny & Zooey*

TONI MORRISON NAMES

Nobel Prize–winning author Toni Morrison, who changed her own name from Chloe to the nickname for her middle name Anthony, is a master of creative character names. Examples:

AJAX	MACON (m)
BELOVED	NEL (f)
DENVER (m)	PALLAS (f)
DORCAS	PECOLA
GUITAR (m)	PILATE (f)
HAGAR (f)	SENECA (f)
HEED (f)	SETHE (f)
JADINE	STAMP (m)
LONE (m)	SULA

Class & Names

The issue of class and names has long been hidden in the closet, a subject that simply wasn't comfortably discussed. In fact, not that long ago, people argued that American names, unlike the British, were free of class markers. Even when it *was* conceded that names might signal class, there was often disagreement about which names were classy and which weren't. But now it seems obvious—a fact confirmed by research in the best-selling book *Freakonomics: A Rogue Economist Explores the Hidden Side of Everything,* by Steven D. Levitt and Stephen J. Dubner, which analyzed distinctly different naming patterns among upper- and lower-class families, parents with different levels of education, and along racial divides—that pronounced disparities do exist.

The Internet has been another factor in illuminating the issue, with bloggers expressing their own ideas of which names have class and—more often—which don't—ideas that vary considerably with geographic areas and ethnicity. The upscale UrbanBaby Web site hosted a recent discussion of low-class names, in which the posters cited Jaden and any name that rhymed with it; Nevaeh and all its cleverly spelled and altered brothers and sisters; along with names that start with *Br* (Britney, Brianna), *Da* (Dakota, Darryl), and *K* (Kylie, Krystal).

Of course, there's a generational/fashion element to the subject of class and names, with lower- (and higher-) class names of one generation giving way to the next. Brenda, Doreen, Tracy, and Wayne, for example, may have been considered lower-class by another generation, but today they're just seen as out of style. To make some broad generalizations, though, it's safe to say that naming your child after a character on a television show is low-class, after a soap opera character lower, and after a reality star (who often seem to be self-named) the lowest of all. Naming your child after a drink is lower class: Bacardi, T'quila, Chardonnay, uh-uh. So is naming your child after a status brand, such as Armani, Lexus, or Cartier.

It's easy enough to make fun of names that don't have class, but more difficult to categorize those that *do*. With parents becoming more conscious of the connection between class and names, names with an obviously classy aura are finding favor. Those in vogue now include, from the current Top 100:

Girls	
ABIGAIL	ELIZABETH
ADDISON	EMMA
ALEXA	FAITH
ALEXIS	GRACE
AMELIA	ISABEL
ARIANNA	JULIA
AUDREY	KATHERINE
AVA	LAURA
AVERY	OLIVIA
BROOKE	PAIGE
CAROLINE	SOPHIA
CHLOE	SOPHIE
CLAIRE	VICTORIA

Boys	OWEN
ADRIAN	SEBASTIAN
ALEXANDER	XAVIER
AUSTIN	
CONNOR	**Either**
ELIJAH	BAILEY
ETHAN	BLAKE
EVAN	CARSON
GABRIEL	CARTER
HENRY	CHASE
IAN	COOPER
JACKSON	LOGAN
JOSIAH	MASON
JULIAN	MORGAN

The letter indicated my much anticipated roommate assignment, typed neatly on a line of its own: Margaret "Margot" Elizabeth Hollinger Graham. All the kids at my public high school had common names like Kim and Jen and Amy. I didn't know anyone with a name like Margot (that silent *t* got me the most) and I definitely didn't know anyone with two middle names.

—Emily Giffin, *Love the One You're With*

Not surprisingly, as names get more popular, they tend to be used less often by upper-class parents. An example of this is Madison, originally a choice of upper-income and -education parents, but once it became megapopular—which is to say, common—it rapidly started a slide down the socioeconomic ladder. When that happens, a name's classy image gets tarnished and newer, shinier names move up to take its place.

If you want to move beyond the favorites to a name with a quieter but more durable brand of class, you might consider the following options. Names overlooked by the masses but with class to spare include:

Girls	GWEN
AGNES	HARRIET
ALICE	HELEN
AMITY	HENRIETTA
ANTONIA	HONOR
ARABELLA	IMOGEN
AUGUSTA	ISADORA
BEATRICE	IVY
CECILIA	JANE
CELIA	JEMIMA
CHARLOTTE	JOCASTA
CLARISSA	JOSEPHINE
CLAUDIA	LOUISE
CLOVER	MARGARET
CONSTANCE	MARIAN
CORA	MARIN
COSIMA	MARTHA
DAPHNE	NATALIA
DINAH	NORA
ELEANOR	PHILIPPA
ELOISE	PORTIA
FELICIA	ROSALIND
FEODORA	ROSEMOND
FLORA	RUTH
FLORENCE	SALLY
FRANCES	SUSANNAH
FREDERICA	TATIANA

VIVIENNE	GILES
WINIFRED	GUY
	HAMISH
Boys	HUGH
ALBERT	IVOR
ANGUS	JASPER
ARTHUR	LEOPOLD
BALTHASAR	LOUIS
BENEDICT	LUCIAN
CHARLES	PATRICK
EDMUND	PETER
EDWARD	PIERCE
FELIX	PIERS
FORD	RALPH
FREDERICK	THOMAS
FRANCIS	VICTOR
GEORGE	WALTER

The Perfect Balance

Time after time we are told by parents—parents who are trying to strike the difficult balance in their lives between parenting and work, the practical and the spiritual—that what they're looking for is a name that's not necessarily unique, but not bizarre either, recognizable but not too popular or trendy, a name that will individualize their child but not create problems or embarrassment for him or her down the road. Finding that perfect balance is difficult, but it's not impossible. The following is a list of names that fit into that golden triangle: they are all real names with real meaning and history, but little likelihood of ever becoming overly trendy—statistically, none of them has been given to more than three hundred babies nationwide in the last year counted. They are names that have just the right mix of distinctiveness, substance, and appeal, and succeed in both fitting in and standing out.

Girls

AMABEL
ANABEL
ANAÏS
BEATRIX
BLANCA
BLYTHE
BREE
BRONTË
BRYONY

CALLA

CELINE

DELIA

DINAH

DIXIE

ESMÉ

GENEVA

GREER

GWYNETH

HONOR

ISADORA

ISLA

JUNO

JUSTINE

LARA

LAUREL

LETICIA

MAISIE

MARIBEL

MAY

MIRABELLA

NATALYA

NELL

OLIVE

PEARL

PORTIA

RHIANNON

RAPHAELA

ROMY

SELINA

SIDONIE

THEA

TYRA

Boys

ABBOTT

ABNER

AMOS

ANDREAS

BARNABY

BENEDICT

BLAISE

CALLUM

CLEMENT

CORMAC

CULLEN

CURRAN

DERMOT

DUNCAN

EDISON

FARRELL

FINIAN

FISHER

FLETCHER

GORDON

HUGH

JAGGER

JUDSON

LARS

LUCIAN

ORSON

OTIS

REEVE
REUBEN
REX
SAMSON
SIMEON

TRUE
TRUMAN
TURNER
YALE

The Nickname Question

First of all, let's establish the fact that when we talk about nicknames, we're not really talking about nicknames, a term that technically refers to those old descriptive, usually derogative slurs like Fatso and Four-Eyes. These, we hope and pray, have pretty much moved off into the well-earned purgatory of Politically Incorrect cruelty. When we refer to nicknames now, we're really talking about pet names or diminutives, like Gracie or Jake.

Many parents have very strong feelings for or against nicknames (as in "My son's name is Andrew, not Andy!"), while for others it's strictly a nonissue. In the more formal, buttoned-up eighties and into the nineties, there was a pervasive trend toward using children's names in full—especially when it came to the standard classics—rather than the more casual forms. But parental insistence on sticking with the undiluted original is easily thwarted. If your eight-year-old Alexandra gets a phone call from a friend asking for Lexie, there's not very much you can do about it, even if you do say, "Hold on, I'll get Alexandra."

If you happen to be among the purist parents who belong to this antinickname contingent, one logical thing for you to do is to seek out a name that seems to be nickname-proof—and we offer a list of just such suggestions on page 114. (Though there is a caveat here too—sometimes a pet form can still be created by simply adding a syllable, with results that may be even worse—just ask Seanie or Brookie.) If what you object to is not nicknames in general but a particular one, you might try choosing a more unusual and distinctive alternative, perhaps an archaic or foreign one, right from the start, before the kids in the playground have a chance to turn Catherine into Cathy. We've unearthed some interesting choices just waiting to be rediscovered.

Of course, you might actually like the energy, friendliness, and informality of a nickname, tailoring your name choice specifically as a path to a short form that you like—picking, for example, Samantha to get to Sam. Or you might use a nickname in and of and for itself—in fact, we see the use of nickname names as such a cool, rising category, that we include it in our So Far Out They're In section on page 41.

In the end, though, whatever your attitude and approach, nicknames seem to have a life of their own no matter how hard you try to control them. So do the best you can to determine the most perfect name for your child, then sit back and relax. Because in the end, the only name you get to pick is the one that goes on the birth certificate.

VINTAGE NICKNAMES

Back when 57 percent of the female population of England was named either Mary, Anne, or Elizabeth, people had to come up with inventive ways of distinguishing one Mary from another—at times even within the same family. So it's hardly surprising that a great diversity of imaginative diminutive names sprang up to solve the problem. Over the years, many of these interesting variations have simply faded away. But some, we think, are worth reconsidering and resurrecting, such as:

Girls

BARRA	*for*	BARBARA
BEAH		BEATRICE
BETTA		ELIZABETH
BRIDEY		BRIDGET
CARO		CAROLINE
CASSIE		CASSANDRA
CATTY		CATHERINE
CHARTY		CHARLOTTE
CILLA		PRISCILLA
DEBS		DEBORAH
DOLA		DOLORES
DORO		DOROTHY
ETTY		HARRIET
FEENY		JOSEPHINE
FLICK		FELICITY
FLOSSIE		FLORENCE
FRANKIE		FRANCES
HATSY		HARRIET
HETTY		HARRIET/HENRIETTA
IBBY		ISABEL
IMMY		IMOGENE
JOSS		JOCELYN
KAT		KATHERINE
KIZZIE		KEZIA
LETTIE		LETITIA
LIBBY		ELIZABETH

LISSIE	ALLISON
LIVVY	OLIVIA
LOTTA/LOTTIE	CHARLOTTE
LULU/LULIE	LOUISE
MAGO	MARGARET
MAGS	MARGARET
MAISIE	MARGARET
MALLY	MARY
MAMIE	MARY
MELIA	AMELIA
MOLL	MARY
NELLIE	ELEANOR/HELEN
NESSA	AGNES/VANESSA
NESSIE	VANESSA
NONIE	NORA
OLLY	OLIVE
OUISA	LOUISE/LOUISA
PATIA	PATRICIA
PIPPA	PHILIPPA
POLLY	MARY
POSY	JOSEPHINE
SUKIE	SUSAN/SUSANNAH
TEDDA	THEODORA
TETTY	ELIZABETH
TILLIE	MATILDA
TORY	VICTORIA
TREE	TERESA
VEVA	GENEVIEVE
VIRGIE	VIRGINIA
VITA	VICTORIA

WINNIE		EDWINA
ZAN		ALEXANDRA

Boys

BENNO	*for*	BENJAMIN
BRAM		ABRAHAM
CHARLOT		CHARLES
CHAZ		CHARLES
CHRISTY		CHRISTOPHER
DAI		DAVID
DEZI		DESMOND
DIX		RICHARD
DOB		ROBERT
DUNN		DUNCAN
FRITZ		FREDERIC
GAZ		GARY
GORE		GORDON
GRAM		GRAHAM
HICK		RICHARD
HITCH		RICHARD
HOB		ROBERT
HODGE		ROGER
JEM		JAMES/JEREMY
JOCK		JOHN
JORI		JORDAN
KIT		CHRISTOPHER
LAURO		LAURENCE
LEX		ALEXANDER
NAB		ABEL
NED		EDWARD

NOLL	OLIVER
PIP	PHILIP
SEB	SEBASTIAN
SIM	SIMON
TAD	THADDEUS
TIP	THOMAS
TOLLY	BARTHOLOMEW
TOMMO	THOMAS
WILLS	WILLIAM
ZAN	ALEXANDER

NO-NICKNAME NAMES

And here, for those of you who hate nicknames, or just hate the idea that someone other than you is going to decide what your child's name is by, say, shortening Allison to Ally, is a list of names that, at least on paper, have no nicknames. (No name is totally invulnerable, however—there's always the danger of some perverse person insisting on calling little April "Ape.")

Girls

APRIL	CHELSEA
AVA	CLAIRE
BLAINE	DAISY
BLAIR	DALE
BLYTHE	DREW
BREE	EDEN
BRETT	EGYPT
BROOKE	FAITH
BRYN	FAY
	GAIL

GREER

HANNAH

HEATHER

HONOR

HOPE

INEZ

INGRID

IRIS

ISLA

IVY

JADE

JOY

LEIGH

MAEVE

MAUVE

MAY

MORGAN

NEVE

NORA

PAIGE

PARIS

PILAR

PIPER

POE

POPPY

PORTIA

RAE

RAIN

RUBY

SAGE

SHEA

SKYE

SLOANE

STARR

TRUE

TYNE

VERVE

VRAI

Boys

AARON

ADAM

AMOS

ASH

AUSTIN

BAILEY

BAIRD

BEAU

BLAKE

BO

BRADY

BRICE

BRIDGE

BROCK

CADE

CASH

CHANCE

CHASE

CLAY

CLEVE

CODY

COLE

CURT	LARS
DALLAS	LLOYD
DAMON	LOCKE
DEAN	LUKE
DREW	LYLE
ELI	MARK
ETHAN	MARLON
FINN	MILES
FLINT	MORGAN
FLYNN	NEMO
FRASER	NEO
GORE	NILES
GRAY	NOAH
GROVER	PALMER
GUY	PIERCE
HARDY	PINE
HARLAN	PRINCE
HARLEY	REED
HARRY	REESE
HERO	REEVE
HUNT	ROSS
IAN	ROY
JUDD	SAWYER
JUDE	SEAN
JUSTICE	SETH
JUSTIN	SHANE
KAI	SLATE
KENT	STEEL
KING	STONE
KIRK	TAJ
KYLE	TATE

THOR   WYATT
TOBY   WYLIE
TRENT   ZANE
WALKER

A nickname is the hardest stone that the devil can throw a man.

—William Hazlitt

Last Names First

Using a surname in first place is as hot a trend as ever, but with some new twists and trends. It's a practice that's gone on for hundreds of years, becoming especially prevalent in this country in the nineteenth century, when upscale brides from prominent families would christen their firstborn sons with their maiden names to symbolize the union of the two families, resulting in names like Broderick Smith and Alcott Brown. Flash forward to the opulent 1980s, and the tradition reemerges, except that parents aren't now necessarily picking names from their own family histories but appropriating other Waspy, impressive-sounding names like Carson and Carter and Parker and Porter for their sons and Whitney and Courtney for their daughters. As a group, these names perfectly captured the spirit of the decade, combining a feminist viewpoint with an image of executive power.

Now the pendulum has swung back, and parents are searching again for names with real, personal meaning; we've progressed from choosing names based on Ralph Lauren–period faux tradition to those that have a genuine connection to family. And the options expand beyond using a mother's maiden name—though more and more parents are doing just that. Shake your own family tree, and you might discover an interesting maternal grandfather's surname or great-great grandmother's maiden name—any of which would impart a valuable, stabilizing sense of family and tradition to your child. This could also be extended to include a cherished family friend, an influential teacher or other mentor. Ethnic names shouldn't be ignored either: After all, if you can name a baby Cooper, why not Cluny or Costa or Chan?

Another surname trend that's being reinvented is using the last names of personal heroes. In the past, parents' focus was on imposing public figures—just look at the presidential surnames that have become recognized as firsts—Jefferson, Madison, Monroe, Jackson, Harrison, Tyler, Taylor, Lincoln, Grant, Truman, Carter, Reagan. This political emphasis has expanded to include more personal heroes, in particular those in the arts. Russell Crowe named his son Tennyson, after his favorite poet, and other celebs have been inspired by W. H. Auden and Samuel Beckett. Musical favorites seem to have particular resonance, be it early rock stars like Presley, Lennon, Jagger, or Hendrix or jazz innovators like Mingus and Miles, or such other musicians as Guthrie, Donovan, Dylan, and Marley. Think about who your own special idols are, and it might lead to a unique choice.

And if you can't find inspiration from the surnames within your own family or among your heroes, here's a selection of fresh surname choices. (For more of the hot occupational surnames, see Names That Work on page 19.)

AMES	BOWEN
ANGELOU	BRAXTON
ARCHER	BROWN
AUDEN	CALLOWAY
BAKER	CALVO
BECKER	CANBY
BELLAMY	CAREW
BLY	CARMICHAEL

CARO

CHENEY

CHRISTO

CLUNY/CLOONEY

CRANE

CROSBY

CULLEN

CURRAN

CURRY

DIAZ

DIX

DUFF

DUFFY

EAMES

EASTON

EGAN

ELLERBY

FERGUSON

FOWLER

GANNON

GETTY

GIBSON

GRAYSON

GUTHRIE

HOLT

JENSEN

KEATON

KEEFE

KEENE

KINSEY

KIRKEBY

LOPEZ

LUNDY

MacLEOD

MAGEE

MAGUIRE

MARLOWE

MERCER

MITCHUM

MOLINA

NASH

NICHOLSON

NIVEN

NORTH

NYE

OAKLEY

OLIVIER

PAISLEY

PALEY

PAXTON

PAZ

PENN

PEREZ

QUARLES

RAFFERTY

RICCI

RIORDAN

ROONEY

RUBIO

SALTER

SCULLY

SMITH

SWEENEY   VIEIRA
TAMAYO   WEST
TATE   WILKIE
THORPE   WINTER
TOLLIVER   YATES
TULLY   ZALE
VANNI

Sex

Whether you're expecting a girl or a boy, or whether you even know the sex of your baby, you're probably talking about the gender implications of names. Unisex names are running rampant, the most fashionable girls' names are either elaborately feminine or decidedly boyish, and the hottest boys' names defy masculine traditions, making the question of gender identity more significant—and more confusing—than ever.

In this section, we take a look at the shifts that have been taking place along the gender divide. In Naming a Daughter, we consider how giving a superfeminine name like Lucinda, a cute girlish name like Lacey, a more serious, womanly name like Laura, all the way to boyish names like Logan or straight-out masculine Lionel is apt to affect your daughter's self-image as well as how others see her.

In Naming a Son, we examine the widely expanding boundaries of baby-boy naming, where for the first time parents are feeling free to be creative and inclusive, drawing not only from the established ranks of biblical and other classics, but the pantheon of Greek gods, foreign lexicons, and newly invented names. We also introduce the category of Metrodude Names, which reflects the sensibility of the cool, hip, stylish urban male.

And in our section on Unisex Names, we take on the state of this growing genre today, to help you navigate the ever-dizzying array of names—Is it a girl? Is it a boy? Does it matter?—that are used for both sexes.

Naming a Daughter

Parents and their little girls have a lot of choices these days, which is both the good news and the bad. Good because our daughters have more freedom than ever to be whoever they want to be and to define femininity any way they choose—the most popular girls' names swing from superfeminine favorites like Olivia to capable grown-up women like Grace to fresh young names like Riley and others that are also fit for boys: Hayden, Avery, Sam. Bad because we're being asked to define it for them, at least in terms of the gender image of their names, before they're even born.

The problem is that you get to pick only one name for your child—well, more than one, but one is what they're known by—and the relative femininity of a girl's name can have long-term consequences. A study of a thousand pairs of twin sisters, for example, showed that girls with more androgynous names, e.g., Alex, are twice as likely to study math and science as they get older than are their sisters with more conventionally feminine names like Isabella, while another study showed that girls with frillier names were more likely to go into more traditionally feminine fields, such as nursing or teaching. Of course, we all know many exceptions to these theories, and in the public eye, there are obvious examples like political powerhouse and Internet entrepreneur

Arianna Huffington and action-film star and human rights activist Angelina Jolie.

Still, parents in search of the right name for their daughters should consider these issues. While the following lists don't cover every girl's name in the lexicon, once you get the idea you should be able to slot any name you find into one of these four categories: Girly-Girl, Womanly, Girlish, or Boyish.

Thinking in terms of gender image can also help in the search for compatible sibling and twin names. Your little Allegra's baby sister might compatibly be named Delilah or Rafaella, while Daisy and Pippa might make a better pair of twin names than Daisy and Bronwen or Annabella.

GIRLY-GIRL NAMES

The following names carry considerable girl power. But today, super-feminine is anything but weak.

ADORA	CAROLINA
ADRIANA	CASSANDRA
ALLEGRA	CELESTIA
ALYSSA	CHRISTABEL
ANGELICA	CLARISSA
ANGELINA	DELILAH
ANNABELLA	DESIREE
ARABELLA	DOMINIQUE
ARIAN(N)A	DOROTHEA
AURORA	ELECTRA
BELINDA	EMMALINE
CAMILLA	EVANGELINA

FELICIA	RAFFAELA
FELICITY	ROSALINDA
GABRIELLA	SABRINA
GEORGIANA	SAMANTHA
ISABELLA	SCARLETT
JOSETTE	SELENA
JULIANA	SERAPHINA/SERAFINA
LARISSA	SERENA
LETITIA	SUSANNAH
LILIANA	SUZETTE
LUCIANA	TABITHA
LUCINDA	TATIANA
MARIETTA	TIFFANY
MELISSA	VALENTINA
MIRABELLE	VALERIA
MONIQUE	VANESSA
PRISCILLA	VENUS

WOMANLY NAMES

These names are clearly feminine but are also serious and grown-up. Though they may be neither cute nor alluring, they're names your daughter may thank you for as she gets older.

ADA	ALANA
ADELAIDE	ALEXA
ADELE	ALEXANDRA
ADRIENNE	ALEXIS
AGATHA	ALICE
AGNES	ALICIA

AL(L)ISON	CHARLOTTE
AMANDA	CHRISTINA
AMELIA	CHRISTINE
ANDREA	CLAIRE
ANGELA	CLAUDIA
ANNA	CONSTANCE
ANNE	CORA
ANNETTE	CORDELIA
ANTONIA	CORNELIA
APRIL	CYNTHIA
AUDREY	DAPHNE
AVA	DEBORAH
BARBARA	DEIRDRE
BEATRICE	DELIA
BERNADETTE	DENISE
BERNICE	DIANA
BIANCA	DIANE
BLANCHE	DINAH
BRIDGET	DONNA
BRONWEN	DORIS
CAITLIN/KAITLYN	DOROTHY
CAMILLE	EDITH
CANDACE	EDNA
CARA	ELAINE
CARLA	ELEANOR
CAROL	ELENA
CAROLINE	ELISE
CATHERINE	ELIZA
CECILY	ELIZABETH
CELESTE	ELLA
CELIA	ELLEN

ENID	HONOR
ESTELLE	HOPE
ESTHER	IDA
ETHEL	IMOGEN
ETTA	INGRID
EUNICE	IRENE
EVA	IRIS
EVE	ISABEL
EVELYN	JACQUELINE
FAITH	JANE
FAY	JANET
FIONA	JANICE
FRANCES	JEAN
GABRIELLE	JOAN
GAIL	JOANNE
GEORGIA	JOCELYN
GERALDINE	JOSEPHINE
GILLIAN	JOY
GINA	JOYCE
GLORIA	JUDITH
GRACE	JULIA
GRETA	JULIANA
GWEN	JULIET
HANNAH	JUNE
HARRIET	JUSTINE
HAZEL	KATE
HELEN	KATHERINE
HELENA	KATHLEEN
HENRIETTA	KAY
HESTER	KIMBERLY
HIL(L)ARY	KIRSTEN

KRISTIN	MARINA
LAILA	MARLENE
LARA	MARTHA
LAURA	MARY
LAUREL	MAUDE
LAUREN	MAURA
LEAH	MAUREEN
LEILA	MAVIS
LENORE	MAXINE
LEONORE	MELANIE
LESLIE	MERCEDES
LILA	MILDRED
LILIAN	MIRANDA
LINDA	MIRIAM
LIZA	MONICA
LORETTA	NAOMI
LORNA	NATALIE
LORRAINE	NATASHA
LOUISA	NICOLE
LOUISE	NORA
LUCILLE	NOREEN
MADELEINE	NORMA
MAEVE	OLIVE
MARA	OLIVIA
MARCIA	PALOMA
MARGARET	PAMELA
MARGO	PATRICIA
MARIA	PAULA
MARIAN	PAULINE
MARIE	PENELOPE
MARIEL	PHILIPPA

PHYLLIS	STEPHANIE
PILAR	SUSAN
RACHEL	SUSANNAH
RAMONA	SUZANNE
REBECCA	SYLVIA
REGINA	TAMAR
RENATA	TAMARA
RENEE	TANYA
RITA	THEODORA
ROCHELLE	T(H)ERESA
ROSALIE	VALERIE
ROSALIND	VERA
ROSE	VERONICA
ROSEMARY	VICTORIA
ROXANNE	VIOLET
SABRINA	VIRGINIA
SANDRA	VIVIAN
SARAH	WANDA
SAVANNAH	WILLA
SELENA	YASMINE
SERENA	YOLANDA
SHEILA	YVONNE
SIMONE	ZANDRA
SONIA	ZARA
SOPHIA	ZORA
STELLA	

MOM NAMES

Names popular in the sixties, seventies, and eighties are today's Mom Names—okay for a thirty-year-old woman, but no longer the feminine image you want for your little girl.

AMY

BETH

CHRIS

CINDY

DANIELLE

DAWN

DEBBIE

ERICA

ERIN

HEATHER

JAMIE

JENNIFER

JESSICA

JUDY

JULIE

KAREN

KATIE

KELLY

KERRY

KIM

KRISTIN

LINDSAY

LISA

LORI

MEGAN

MELISSA

MICHELLE

ROBIN

SHANNON

SHARON

STACY

TAMMY

TARA

TRACY

WENDY

GIRLISH NAMES

These are cute and girlish names that have obvious appeal for when your daughter is a baby, child, or even a teen. Many of them—Annabel, Chloe, Maggie—hold on to their youthful energy into adulthood as well, but some others—Darlene, Gretchen, Sherry—though they may have started out as feminine and frilly as the rest, are now, alas, seen as Grandma names.

ALI/ALLIE	EDIE
AMY	ELLIE
ANNABEL	EMILY
ANNIE	EMME/EMMY
BEA	ESMÉ
BECCA	FANNY
BESS	GIGI
BILLIE	GRETCHEN
BONNIE	HALEY/HAYLEY
CALEIGH	HALLIE
CALLIE	HEIDI
CARRIE	HOLLY
CASS(IE)	JENNA
CAT	JENNY
CHELSEA	JILL
CHLOE	JOSIE
CHRISTA	JULIE
CLEMENTINE	KATIE
COCO	KELLY
COLETTE	KELSEY
COLLEEN	KERRY
COREY	KIM
DAISY	KINSEY
DANI	KIRSTIE
DARLA	KITTY
DARLENE	KRISTY
DOLLY	LACEY

LIBBY	PIPPA
LILY	POLLY
LIV	POPPY
LIZZIE	ROSIE
LUCY	RUBY
LULU	SADIE
MADDIE	SALLY
MAGGIE	SHERRY
MAISIE	SOPHIE
MAMIE	TAFFY
MAY	TESS
MEGAN	TESSA
MERRY	TILLIE
MIA	TINA
MISSY	TORY
MOLLY	WENDY
NELL(IE)	ZOE
PANSY	

BOYISH NAMES

Over the past few decades, girls have been moving steadily into the boys' baby-naming territory, adopting names that range from Jordan all the way to George. Here are some choices being used for girls today. For more, check out the Unisex Names on page 151.

AIDAN	AVERY
ALEX	BAILEY
AUGUST	BLAIR
AUSTEN	BLAKE

BRADLEY	JADEN
BRADY	JALEN
BRETT	JAMESON
BRINLEY	JAMIE
BRODY	JAY
BRYN	JESSIE
CARTER	JO
CASEY	JODY
CLAUDE	JORDAN
CORY	KAI
DALLAS	KIT
DARREN	LANE
DARRYL	LEE
DELANEY	LEIGHTON
DEVON	LENNON
DONOVAN	LENNOX
DREW	LOGAN
DUSTIN	LONDON
DYLAN	LOU
ELLERY	MARLEY
ELLIOT	MASON
EMERSON	MILAN
FINLAY	MONET
FINN	MORGAN
FLANNERY	PARIS
FLYNN	PARKER
FRANKIE	PEYTON
GLENN	PRESLEY
HARLEY	QUINN
HAYDEN	RAY
IZZY	RILEY

RORY	SYDNEY
RYAN	TRUE
SAM	

MANNISH NAMES

Sam still too feminine for you? Then you might want to choose a name straight from the list others might consider off-limits for girls. And the truth is, dusty male names like Stanley and Murray do seem new and fresh when applied to girls.

ARTHUR	MICHAEL
BRADLEY	MURRAY
CURTIS	NEIL
ELLISON	OWEN
IRA	RALEIGH
JAMES	ROY
JEREMY	STANLEY
LAWRENCE	WALKER
LIONEL	

Naming a Son

This is a great time to be naming a son. Never before have there been as many options, approaches, and individual names for boys as there are now.

Unlike previous generations of parents, whose choice was basically between James and John, David and Daniel, Richard and Robert or, if they were a little more daring, Ryan or Brian, the recent explosion of male name choices has permanently changed that scenario. Yes, if you're a traditionally minded baby namer, you can still choose from the roster of classic all-boy Anglo-Saxon and biblical alternatives, names that project a straightforward, unequivocally masculine image, sure to please parents and in-laws alike. They may not set off sparks of excitement, but these are names that will serve a son well for a lifetime. Most of them come equipped with lighter nicknames for the early years, along with a lifelong warranty that will last through college, career, and beyond.

But there's also an endless array of other kinds of names that present more nuanced male images.

One of these is what we're calling Powerboy names, as reflected in the current pervasive Dark Knight–Iron Man superhero culture. These are for parents looking for a name that projects superstrength, an almost larger-than-life, invulnerable aura of masculinity. These are the most muscular, if not macho, of names. Included in this category are the names of powerful Greek and Roman gods like Ares and Zeus, strong word names like Cannon and Maverick, and the increasingly popular short, sharp, one-syllable thunderbolt names like Slate and Stone—all names that have never and will never be used for girls.

At the other end of that spectrum are the Metrodude names, that newly defined gender of the urban male who's cool, hip, urban, trendy, stylish, sensitive, artistic, creative, and confident, on the cutting edge of fashion. A straight man in touch with his feminine side, he not only reads *GQ*, he might well appear in its pages. The names we include in this category are the hippest of the hip, the coolest of the cool. Also adding to the inventory of male choices are foreign imports from Ireland, Italy, Spain, Russia, and other cultures—a constantly expanding band of émigrés, appealing to parents looking for a touch of international panache. But the biggest element of change in naming boys is the spirit of creativity and adventure of the modern parent. Why be limited to the ho-hum Jason, when you can have your pick of Jayson, Jayden, Jaylen, Jase, or Jace (all of which rank on the current popularity list)—or even create your own unique version?

Several factors have contributed to the loosening of the strictures on boys' names. For one thing, in the past, it was fathers who had the greater input and interest in the naming of their sons, often with a somewhat rigid concern for carrying on family traditions and presenting a virile image—it wasn't unusual for Dad to pick the boys' names in the family and Mom to choose the girls'. And to some degree this attitude persists. More boys than girls are still given the top-ranked names, though the figures are beginning to equalize, as the dichotomy between our expectations for sons and daughters diminishes. As dads become more involved and invested in child-rearing and are exposed to the strengths of girls and sensitivities of boys, stereotypical attitudes toward what girls' and boys' names should imply change as well.

Then, too, the whole climate of baby naming in general has altered dramatically, as choices have become such a focus of interest, from the celebrity culture on down. There has evolved a certain amount of peer pressure and implied judgment, as in: "The Andersons named their son Paul? Couldn't they come up with anything more interesting?" The rampant critical discussion buzzing along the Internet about not only Gwen Stefani's choices but sister-in-law Sue's has led to a general striving to find a name—for boys as well as girls—that will make a favorable impression on the virtual Name Jury. This factor, coupled with the "I-want-my-child-to-stand-out" desire, has also fueled the search for a more distinctive name. Boys now have their own trends and trendlets, like the myriad names rhyming with Aidan, names ending in *en* and *er,* hard-edged single-syllable names and names with a hard *k* sound—but spelled interchangeably beginning with *k* or *c.*

On the other hand, one factor that has diminished the pool of boys' names is that so many once all-male names have increasingly become not only shared with girls, but sometimes overtaken by them. Nowadays you may have to peek inside the diaper to see if little Avery or Ryan or Riley or Reese is a boy or a girl. Even more conventional male names that seemed impervious to a female takeover, such as James and George and Noah—not to mention nickname names Charlie and Sam—have sneaked onto baby girls' birth certificates. And while it may not seem fair, the fact is that once a name is appearing regularly in the female column, it usually becomes less feasible for a boy. But there are signs that this is changing—as seen in the Metrodude section.

What follows are lists of Powerboy Names, All-Boy Classics, Biblical Boys, and Metrodude Names. For more ideas on naming your son, see the lists of Names That Work (page 19), Starbabies (page 9), Baby

Gods & Goddesses (page 44), But Seriously . . . (page 73), International Ideas (page 191)—plus all the other great options scattered throughout the book, as well as on our Web site, nameberry.com.

POWERBOY NAMES

Here, flexing their muscles, are the names for your little superhero:

ACE	CADE
ACHILLES	CAESAR
ANCHOR	CAIN
APOLLO	CALE/KALE
ARIES	CANNON
ARROW	CARL
ATLAS	CASE
AXEL	CASH
BIX	CHANCE
BLADE	CHASE/CHACE
BLAZE	CLINT
BOGART	COLE
BOND	COLT
BOONE	CONAN
BRAWLEY	CREW
BRECK	CRUZ
BRICK	CURT/KURT
BRIDGE	DART
BROCK	DASH
BRONCO	DEUCE
BRUNO	DOLPH
BUCK	DRAKE

DRAVEN	KING
DUFF	KNOX
DUKE	LEITH
DURANGO	LENNOX
EAGLE	LEX
FITZ	LINK
FLINT	LOCKE
FORD	LODGE
FORT	LOTHAR
FOX	MACE
GABLE	MAGNUS
GAGE	MANNIX
GERONIMO	MARS
GOLIATH	MAVERICK
GORE	MAXIMUS
GRANITE	MEAD
GUNNER	NASH
HARLEY	NAVARONE
HAWK	NEO
HERCULES	NERO
HITCH	NIGHT
HOLT	ORION
HOUSTON	PACE
HUGH	PIERCE
HUNT	PIKE
HYDE	POSEIDON
IGOR	RACER
JAGGER	RAM
JET/JETT	RANGER
KEEN	REBEL
KILLIAN	REEF

REEVE	THORNE
RENO	TIGER
REX	TITAN
RIDGE	TITUS
ROCCO	TOR
ROCK	TRACE
ROCKET	TRENT
ROGUE	UZI
ROPER	VICTOR
RYDER	VIGGO
SCORPIO	VINCE
SEAL	VLAD
SHOOTER	VULCAN
SLATE	WOLF
STEEL/STEELE	ZADE
STONE	ZANE
TATE	ZEUS
TEX	ZINC
THANE	ZOLTAN/ZOLTEN
THOR	

Words have meaning and names have power.

—Author unknown

ALL-BOY CLASSICS

Here, choices from the lexicon of timeless traditional boys' names:

ALAN	ALEC
ALBERT	ALEXANDER

ALFRED	JOSHUA
ANDREW	JUSTIN
ANTHONY	LAWRENCE
ARTHUR	LEO
BENJAMIN	LEWIS/LOUIS
CARL	LINCOLN
CHARLES	LIONEL
CHRISTOPHER	LUCAS
CLIFFORD	LUKE
DANIEL	MARK
DAVID	MARTIN
DOUGLAS	MATTHEW
EDWARD	MAX
ERIC	MICHAEL
FRANK	NATHAN
FREDERICK	NATHANIEL
GEORGE	NEAL/NEIL
GERALD	NED
GORDON	NICHOLAS
GREGORY	NORMAN
HARRY	OLIVER
HARVEY	PATRICK
HENRY	PAUL
HUGH	PETER
JACK	PHILIP
JAMES	RALPH
JEFFREY	RAYMOND
JEREMY	RICHARD
JOHN	ROBERT
JONATHAN	ROGER
JOSEPH	RONALD

ROY	TIMOTHY
RUSSELL	VICTOR
SEBASTIAN	VINCENT
SIMON	WALTER
STEWART/STUART	WARREN
THEODORE	WILLIAM
THOMAS	ZACHARY

BIBLICAL BOYS

Parents in search of a solid name for their sons have always looked to the Bible as a rich source of inspiration. As a group of biblical names in each generation becomes widely popular, another will come along to take its place. In recent times, Joshua, Adam, and Samuel, for example, have made room for current fresher-sounding favorites such as Caleb, Ethan, and Asher. Here, a list of Old Testament possibilities, from the familiar to the more obscure:

AARON	ASA
ABEL	ASHER
ABIEL	AZRIEL
ABIJAH	BARAK
ABNER	BARUCH
ABRAHAM	BENJAMIN
ABSALOM	BOAZ
ADLAI	CALEB
AHAB	ELEAZAR
AHAZ	ELI
AMOS	ELIAS
ARAM	ELIHU

ELIJAH	JONAH
ELISHA	JOSEPH
EMANUEL	JOSIAH
EPHRAIM	JUDAH
ESAU	LEVI
ETHAN	MALACHI
EZEKIEL	MICAH
EZRA	MOSES
GABRIEL	NATHAN
GIDEON	NATHANIEL
HIRAM	NOAH
ISAAC	OBADIAH
ISAIAH	OMAR
ISHMAEL	PHINEAS
JABAL	RAPHAEL
JABEZ	REUBEN
JADON	RUFUS
JAEL	SAMSON
JARED	SAMUEL
JAVAN	SAUL
JEDIDIAH	SETH
JEREMIAH	SIMEON
JESSE	SIMON
JETHRO	SOLOMON
JOAB	TOBIAS
JOACHIM	ZACHARIAH
JOEL	ZEBEDIAH

METRODUDE NAMES

There's a new gender class of boys' names that moves beyond any of the older categories. Distinctly male yet not traditionally so, serious yet not conventional, unthreatened by a touch of the feminine, these are among the most popular boys' names today. Do they reflect a change in the zeitgeist when it comes to male image? We think so. Now that young dads are unashamedly interested in style and cooking and in being hands-on parents, now that young moms feel more confident about the importance of their roles both in the world and at home, parents are more comfortable with boys' names that reinvent the gender categories.

Of course, this has been happening for some time with girls' names, too, but the old rule was that as soon as a male name crossed into the girl's territory—note Ashley, Courtney, Blair—it became off-limits for boys. But that's happening less and less now, with parents seemingly unconcerned as names like Ryan and Jaden start being used for girls. They're still very much on the list for boys, too, and we see that as yet another positive step for both the culture and for baby names.

Not all of these names are also used for girls. What they do share, though, is a modern, sophisticated, metrosexual-meets-dude image. These are not your father's baby names, and not your father's image of what little boys are made of. This new generation of boys' names includes:

ADRIAN	BALTHAZAR
AIDEN/AIDAN	BARNABY
ALEXIS	BEECH
ANDERSON	BIRCH
ASH	BLAISE
ASHTON	BLAKE
AUSTIN	BRADY
AVERY	BRANCH

BRANDON	CONOR/CONNOR
BRAXTON	COOPER
BRAYDEN/BRADEN	CORBIN
BRENDAN	COREY
BRENNAN	CRANE
BRIAN/BRYAN	CRISPIN
BROCK	DAKOTA
BRODY	DALTON
BROOKS	DAMIAN
BRYSON	DANE
CADE	DANTE
CADEN/KADEN	DAVIS
CALE	DAWSON
CALEB/KALEB	DAX
CALVIN	DECLAN
CAMDEN	DERRICK
CAMERON	DEVIN/DEVON
CARSON	DEXTER
CARTER	DILLON/DYLAN
CASH	DONOVAN
CERULEAN	DREW
CHANCE	DUSTIN
CHASE	EASTON
CHRISTIAN	ELLIOT
CLAYTON	EMILIO
CODY	ENZO
COHEN	EVAN
COLBY	EWAN
COLE	FABIAN
COLIN	FELIX
COLTON	FINN

FROST	JEX
FYFE	JOAQUIN
GARRETT	JORDAN
GAVIN	JULIAN
GRAHAM	JUSTICE
GRANT	JUSTIN
GRAY	KAI
GRAYSON	KEEGAN
GRIFFIN	KIAN
HARRISON	KIER
HAYDEN	KINGSTON
HENDRIX	KYLE
HOLDEN	KYLER
HOUSTON	LAIRD
HUCK	LANDON
HUDSON	LANE
HUGO	LEIF
HUNTER	LENNON
INDIO	LIAM
INIGO	LINCOLN
IVAN	LOGAN
JACE	LORCAN
JACKSON	LUCA
JAGGER	LUKAS
JASON	MADDOX
JASPER	MAGNUS
JAX	MALIK
JAYDEN/JADEN	MARCUS
JAYLEN	MASON
JEFFERSON	MAX
JEREMY	MAXWELL

MICAH	SKYLER
MILES	SMITH
MILO	TAJ
MORGAN	TANNER
NOLAN	TATE
OAK	TENNYSON
OMAR	TRACK
ORSON	TRAVIS
OSCAR	TRENT
OWEN	TRENTON
OZ	TREVOR
PARKER	TREY
PEYTON	TRIG
PRESTON	TRIP
QUENTIN	TRISTAN
QUINN	TROY
RAFAEL	TUCKER
RAFE	TY
RAUL	TYLER
REMY	TYSON
ROMAN	WESLEY
ROWAN	WESTON
RYLAN	WYATT
SAWYER	XANDER
SEAN	XAVIER
SEBASTIAN	ZANE
SHANE	ZENO
SILAS	ZION

Unisex Names

Unisex names have become only more, not less, acceptable for both boys and girls over time, with choices for both moving toward the middle. Sometimes, all that distinguishes the boys' version from the girls' is the spelling, with the substitution of the more feminine-appearing letter *y* for the *e* in the more conventional spelling used for a boy.

The increasing use of unisex names reflects the overall blurring of gender boundaries. Girls are earning their college degrees, entering professional schools, and forging serious careers in record numbers. Boys, meanwhile, are leaving the old macho stereotypes behind as they grow up to become hands-on parents, full emotional partners, more interested in grooming and style. Modern parents want their children similarly to embrace the best of life without regard to old-time gender divisions and rules—and that includes names.

In the sections on Naming a Daughter and Naming a Son, we detailed the names used at the boyish end for girls and on the more androgynous side for boys. Here's the full complement of most popular names used for babies of both sexes, with spelling variations.

ADDISON, Addisyn   ALEX, Alix
AIDAN, Aiden   ALEXIS, Alexus

ALI

AMERICA, Amerika

ANGEL

ARMANI

ASA, Aza

ASHTON, Ashtyn

ASPEN

AUBREY, Aubree

AUDEN

AUGUST

AUSTEN, Austin, Austyn

AVALON

AVERY

BAILEY, Baylee, Bayley, Bayleigh

BELLAMY

BERKELEY

BLAINE

BLAIR

BLAKE

BRADEN, Braeden, Brayden

BRADY

BRAXTON

BRETT

BRILEY, Brylee, Bryleigh

BRODY

BROOKLYN, Brooklynn

BROOKS, Brookes

BRYCE, Brice

BRYSON, Brycen

CADE, Kade

CADEN, Kaden

CALE, Kale

CAMDEN

CAMERON, Camryn

CARSON, Carsen

CARTER

CASEY, Cayce, Kaycee

CASSIDY

CHARLESTON

CHASE, Chace

CHRISTIAN

COLBY

COLTON

CONOR, Conner, Connor

CORBIN

DAKOTA

DALLAS

DECLAN, Declyn

DELANEY

DEVON, Devin, Devyn

DREW, Dru

DYLAN, Dillon

EASTON

ELIOT, Elliot, Elliott

ELLERY

EMERSON

EVAN

FINLEY, Finlay

FINN

FLYNN

GENESIS

GLENN, Glen

GRAY, Grey

GRAYSON

HARLEY, Harleigh

HARPER

HAVEN

HAYDEN, Haden

HEAVEN

HUDSON

INDIGO

JADEN, Jayden, Jadon, Jadyn

JAGGER

JALEN, Jalyn, Jaylen

JAMESON, Jamison

JAMIE, Jayme

JAX

JESSE, Jessie

JETSON

JETT, Jet

JORDAN, Jordyn

JUNO, Junot

JUSTICE, Justis

KAI, Cai, Ky

KEATON, Keeton

KEEGAN, Keagan

KEIL, Kiel

KELLEN

KELSEY

KENDALL

KENNEDY

KINGSTON

KYLE

KYLER

LAKE

LANDON

LANDRY

LANE, Layne

LEE, Lea, Leigh

LENNON

LENNOX

LEXIS, Lexus

LOGAN

LONDON

LOREN, Lauren, Lauryn

LUCA

MARLEY

MASON

MICAH, Mica

MISHA, Mischa

MONTANA

MORGAN

NICO, Niko

NOAH, Noe

NORTH

OCEAN

OWEN

PARIS

PARKER

PAZ

PEYTON, Payton

PRESLEY

PUMA

QUINN

RAIN, Rainn, Rayne

RAY, Rae

REAGAN, Regan

REED, Reid

REESE, Rhys

REEVE

REMY, Remi

RILEY, Rylee, Ryleigh

RIPLEY

ROCKET

ROMY

RONAN, Ronin

RORY

ROWAN, Rohan, Rowen

RYAN, Rian

RYDER, Rider

SAGE

SAILOR, Saylor

SAM

SASHA, Sacha

SAWYER

SCOUT

SEAN, Shaun, Shawn

SHEA, Shay, Shaye

SHILOH

SIERRA, Ciera, Cierra

SKY, Skye

SKYLER, Skylar, Schuyler

SLOANE

SPENCER, Spenser

STORY

TAJ

TATE

TAY, Taye

TAYLOR, Tayler

TOBY

TRACE

TRISTAN

TRUE

TYLER

TYSON

WEST

WESTON

WYLIE

ZANE

ZEN, Xen

ZION

UNISEX STARBABIES

| AUDEN (girl) | Noah Wyle |
| (boy) | Amber Valletta |

BAILEY (girl)	Scott Baio, Melissa Etheridge, Stella McCartney
(boy)	Anthony Edwards, Tracey Gold
BAYLEE (boy)	Brian Littrell
BAYLEY (girl)	Teri Polo
CHARLIE (boy)	Mimi Rogers, Soledad O'Brien
(girl)	Rebecca Romijn & Jerry O'Connell
ELIOT (boy)	Robert De Niro
ELLIOTT (girl)	Alexandra Wentworth & George Stephanopoulos
EVAN (girl)	Jon Heder
(boy)	Jenny McCarthy
FINLEY (girl)	Angie Harmon & Jason Sehorn, Lisa Marie Presley
(boy)	Chris O'Donnell, Holly Marie Combs
FINN (girl)	Jane Leeves
(boy)	Christy Turlington & Ed Burns
HARPER (girl)	Martie (Dixie Chicks) Maguire, Alexandra Wentworth & George Stephanopoulos, Lisa Marie Presley
(boy)	Laura Allen
HUDSON (girl)	James Barbour
(boy)	Marcia Gay Harden, Harvey Keitel
JAGGER (girl)	Soleil Moon Frye
(boy)	Lindsay Davenport, Brett Scallions
JUDAH (girl)	Ziggy Marley
(boy)	Lucy Lawless
KAI (girl)	Donald Trump, Jr.
(boy)	Jennifer Connelly
LUCA (girl)	Jennie Garth
(boy)	Colin Firth, Vincent D'Onofrio
LUCKY (girl)	Cedric the Entertainer
(boy)	Damon Dash

MASON (girl)	Kelsey Grammer
(boy)	Cuba Gooding, Jr., Laura San Giacomo, Melissa Joan Hart
NOAH (girl)	Billy Ray Cyrus
(boy)	Scott Weiland
OWEN (girl)	Michelle Branch
(boy)	Noah Wyle, Ricki Lake
PARIS (girl)	Michael Jackson
(boy)	Pierce Brosnan, Blair Underwood
RAIN (girl)	Marisol Nichols
(boy)	Corey Hart
RILEY (girl)	Norah O'Donnell
(boy)	David Lynch, Holly Marie Combs, Katie Wagner
SAGE (girl)	Lance Henriksen, Toni Collette
(boy)	Tracey Gold
SAM (girl)	Denise Richards, Tiger Woods
(boy)	Emily Mortimer
SCOUT (girl)	Tom Berenger
(boy)	Tai Babilonia
SPENCER (girl)	Kelsey Grammer, Debbe Dunning
(boy)	Cynthia McFadden, Gena Lee Nolan, Cuba Gooding, Jr.

Girl-Boy Name Equality

Once upon a time, there were girls' names that sprang from their male master versions: Geraldine from Gerald, for instance, or in more modern times Danielle from Daniel.

But there's a newer brand of female-male name equality: Names that belong distinctly to one sex or another and may not even spring from the same root, yet are related in sound and feel.

Many of today's most stylish names come in matching girl and boy versions. The advantage: If you find a name you like, you can alter it by a few letters and come up with a variation that works for the other sex. The downside: Once you name a daughter Eliza, you can hardly name her little brother Elijah.

Here's a selection of modern female-male equivalent names:

Addison—Edison

Alexis—Alexander

Arianna—Adrian

Ashley—Ashton or Asher

Audrey—Auden

Ava or Ada—Aiden

Cadence—Caden

Camryn—Camden

Chloe—Cole

Delaney—Dylan

Eliza—Elijah

Ella or Ellie—Eli

Emma—Emmett

Eva—Evan

Finlay—Finn

Gabriella—Gabriel

Grace—Grayson

Hayley—Hayden

Isabella—Isaac or Isaiah

Jada—Jaden

Jasmine—Jackson

Julia—Julian

Katelyn—Kaden

Kayla—Caleb

Kylie—Kyle

Leah—Liam

Lucy—Luke or Lucas

Madison or Macy—Mason

Makayla—Malachy

Miley—Milo

Natalie—Nathan or Nathaniel

Nora—Noah

Olivia—Oliver

Patience—Peyton

Reese—Reed or Reeve

Rylee—Ryan

Samantha—Samuel

Taylor—Tyler

Thea—Theo

Willa or Willow—Will

Tradition

Despite all the talk of innovation and trendiness, tradition still plays a major role in the choice of names. For many, the quest for novelty and creativity is coupled with a search for personal meaning, embracing family history and ethnic identity. And lots of the most exciting and appealing new names can be found by digging into your own past or cultural background.

A capsule history of American baby naming provides insight into trends over time, and our carefully researched section on African-American names deconstructs these often misunderstood names that have evolved over the centuries as a distinctive part of our culture.

We also offer some surprising saints' names (including Ava and Aidan) to prove that such choices don't have to be stodgy or boring, and a short history of Jewish-American naming, lists of Hebrew and mixed-marriage suggestions, and an update of our popular Kosher Curve feature, plus lists of names that are popular in Europe but little known here.

Finally, this section offers advice on a number of thorny family issues—everything from naming siblings, middle and surnames, and how to deal with unwanted advice from well-meaning family and friends.

Trends Over Time

In the centuries since the earliest settlers arrived on our shores, our inventory of names has grown from the limited stock of Anglo-Saxon standard names—John and William and Mary and Elizabeth—that they brought with them, to a big stewpot incorporating flavors from different immigrant cultures spiced with names created on our own native soil. Looking back over our naming history can provide inspiration to today's baby namer.

THE EARLY YEARS

Although the first English-speaking settlement—the Raleigh Colony—soon vanished, we're lucky enough to have some of their name records. Of the ninety-nine men who settled there, twenty-three were named John, fifteen Thomas, and ten William, plus a sprinkling of biblical names. The proportion was similar on the *Mayflower,* though there were also passengers named Resolved, Love, and Wrestling. When it came time for the settlers to name their own offspring, some of the old traditional standards faded in favor of Biblical Names, from both the Old and New Testaments. The Good Book was scrutinized in the search for names of righteous figures, parents strongly believing that such names could shape the character of their children. Biblical names ranged from the common—Sarah, Rachel, Rebecca, Samuel, Benjamin—to the more extreme, such as Eliphalet and Bezaleel. In their pursuit of ever-more-upright, upstanding names, the Puritans went even further, choosing meaningful Virtue Names—in fact, Thankful was one of the most common names for New England girls before 1750.

Here are some of the names used in colonial times—biblical, virtue, and others—that are viable choices for today's babies:

Girls

ABIGAIL
CHARITY
COMFORT
DINAH
ELIZA
HONOR
JANE
JEMIMA
KETURAH
LYDIA
MERCY
PRISCILLA
PRUDENCE
SELAH
SUSANNA

Boys

ABIJAH
ABRAHAM
BOAZ
EBENEZER
ELIHU
ELIJAH
EZEKIEL
EZRA
GIDEON
JEDEDIAH
JETHRO
JOSIAH
MICAH
MOSES
OBADIAH
SOLOMON
TOBIAH
ZEDEKIAH

Toward the end of the seventeenth century, there was an influx of European immigrants, adding more diversity to the mix. Names such as Frederick (German), Andrew and Alexander (Scottish), Patrick and Patricia (Irish) became integrated into American nomenclature, biblical names began to recede, replaced by such newly popular names as Charles, George, Francis, and Augustus, royal imports like Charlotte and Caroline, in addition to a revival of the Robert-Henry-Edward breed. Another trend that started to take hold (and still thrives today) is that of using surnames as firsts, which led to such innovations as Curtis, Everett, Franklin, Grant, Marshall, Otis, Randolph, Warren, and Wayne. Yet another novelty at this time was the legitimizing of nicknames. For centuries girls and boys had been called by pet forms; now those diminutives became the names they were christened with, causing an explosion of new girls' names. Among the newly sanctioned examples were:

ABBY	JESSIE
ANNIE	KITTY
BESS	LETTY
BETSY	LUCY
BETTY	LULU
CARRIE	MAISIE
DAISY	MAMIE
ELSIE	MILLY
HATTIE	MINNIE
JENNY	NANCY

NELL	SALLY
PEGGY	WINNIE
SADIE	

The eighteenth century also saw upper-class parents using Latinized forms of female names. Mary was now apt to be called Maria, and others like Sophia, Anna, Juliana, and Cecilia came into widespread use.

THE NINETEENTH CENTURY

There were several trends that broadened naming choices during this period. Some parents turned to the classics and used Homer, Horatio, and Horace as namesakes, while others were inspired by Anglo-Saxon sagas to name their sons and daughters such chivalrous names as Arthur, Alfred, and Harold, Enid, Edith, and Elaine. From Sir Walter Scott novels came other heroic names (which might not sound so now)—Kenneth, Donald, and Ronald, and from other romances, Lavinia, Clarissa, and Rosalind. Flower names blossomed—Rose, Violet, Iris—and gem names sparkled—Pearl, Opal, Ruby—not to mention the months April, May, and June. Yet another trend for girls was the widespread feminization of male names: Henrietta, Josephine, Charlotte, Edwina.

For boys, there was an accelerated use of the strictly American "Junior" form, a large proportion of boys being named for their fathers. Another rich source was the ranks of aristocratic surnames of the English and Scottish nobility, with boy babies now being called Barry, Craig, Harvey, Herbert, Howard, Sidney, and Stanley. As time went on, and as children's position became more elevated in society, more attention was paid to the choice of their names—a mild foretaste of what was to follow in the succeeding centuries.

THE TWENTIETH CENTURY

All the movements mentioned above gradually coalesced to form an almost infinite number of names available to the prospective parent at the turn of the twentieth century. Classics William, John, Charles, and James continued to dominate the boys' list, but for girls, though Mary still held first place (as it would until 1950), there were new entries on the Top 10 list, including Ruth, Margaret, Dorothy, Mildred, and Frances. The 1920s and 1930s saw some major shifts. For the first time, media stars were affecting baby naming, as in Jean, Marion, Myrna, Shirley, and Virginia. Other female fads included names ending in *s* (Doris, Phyllis, Lois), Irish and Gallic names ending in *een* and *ene* (Maureen, Kathleen, Arlene, Marlene), and the even more fashionably French Annette, Paulette, and Nanette. One of the hottest trends for both sexes was what you might call Freckle-Faced "Our Gang" Comedy Names that came complete with high-voltage energy, button noses, and overbites. These would include:

ANDY	OLLIE
BARNEY	PATSY
BETSY	PEGGY
DEXTER	PENNY
GINNY	POLLY
HOMER	SALLY
KITTY	TRUDY
MARGIE	WILBUR
MICKEY	WILLIS
NED	WINNIE

By the 1940s, some of the fustier feeling names had fallen off the Top 10, to be replaced by Ronald, David, Carol, Joan, Judith—and

Linda, the fresh-sounding name that would finally topple Mary from first place. There were also new, more sophisticated, slightly exotic names for kids whose parents envisioned them triumphing over the Great Depression and growing up to wear glamorous satin gowns, drink martinis, and dangle cigarette holders. (No one could foresee that these same names would become the standard TV sitcom Mom and Dad names of the near future.) Birth certificates of this era were likely to display girls' names like Anita and Rita, Pamela and Sandra, and boys called Alan, Mitchell, Roger, and Russell.

Post-World-War-II America was a time of bubbling optimism and a major baby boom, which spawned a whole new generation of cuter, younger, glossier names for kids who would play with Betsy Wetsy dolls and watch Howdy Doody. Linda had leaped into the number-one spot and Sharon and Karen were neck and neck at number nine, with other more modern-sounding girls' names like Amy, Brenda, Cheryl, Donna, Julie, Kim, Lisa, and Wendy popping onto the list. For boys, Robert was still in top place, but Michael, a biblical name that had been out of favor for two hundred years, catapulted to second place, with other new names appearing, including Gary, Dennis, Douglas, and Bruce. What we call Beach Boy Names, a group of superkeen monikers, hit the shores in the late fifties and early sixties, the personification of surfer machismo. Riding the waves were such righteous dudes as:

BRAD	RICK
CHAD	SCOTT
DARREN	TAD
DARRYL	THAD
DEAN	TODD
DUANE/DWAYNE	TROY
GLENN	WAYNE
LANCE	

It was in the fifties that TV began to have a noticeable impact on names, for one thing reintroducing a whole posse of long-forgotten Western handles like Jason, Josh, Jesse, and Jeremy.

An even greater name revolution came during the Age of Aquarius, when gender stereotypes were being reexamined as men grew their hair long and women (at least metaphorically) burned their bras; clothing became unisex, and so did names: the Kellys, Kerrys, Coreys, Caseys, Jamies, Jodys, Staceys, and Traceys in the sandbox could be either boys or girls. In an atmosphere of "Do your own thing" and "Let it all hang out," new names were invented, and the spelling of traditional names became a contest of creativity: Karen was now Caryn and Laurie had become Lori—the latter just one of a large group of Nickname Names that included Cindy, Mindy, Marnie, Marcy, Tammy, and Toni.

The sixties was also the era of invented Hippie Names—not unlike the word and nature names that are making a comeback right now (see Style section). Among the grooviest flower-child names, forebears of today's word names, were:

AMERICA	HARMONY
BREEZE	JUNIPER
CAT	LEAF
CAYENNE	LIBERTY
CHE	LIGHT
CHINA	LOVE
CLOUD	MEADOW
CLOVER	MOON
COYOTE	MYSTIC
DOVE	OCEAN
ECHO	PEACE
FEATHER	PHOENIX
GYPSY	RAIN

RAINBOW	SPRING
RAVEN	STAR
RIVER	STARSHINE
SEAGULL	STORM
SEASON	SUMMER
SEQUOIAH	SUNSHINE
SIERRA	TRUE
SILVER	VENUS
SKY	WELCOME

At this time, too, with the rise of Black Nationalism and ethnic pride, African-American naming patterns started to sharply diverge from the general population, broadening a long tradition of seeking distinctive names. Now, black parents began looking to Muslim and African sources for their children's names, and also took the roots of those native names and made them their own. In New York, from 1973 to 1975, for example, 31 percent of black girls and 19 percent of boys were given unique names. This surge of creativity would have a profound influence on baby names across the board. (For a more comprehensive treatment of black names, see African-American Naming Traditions, pages 171–176.)

The 1970s saw a revival of Pioneer Names, such as:

ANNIE	JASON
BEAU	JEB
BECKY	JED
BETSY	JENNY
CARRIE	JESSE/JESSIE
CASSIE	JOSH
CLAY	KIT
CLINT	KITTY
CODY	LUKE

MAGGIE	TESS
SARA	ZEB
SETH	

At the same time there was a widespread return of Old Testament Names—Adam, Benjamin, Jason, Samuel, Jonathan, Rachel, Rebecca, and Sarah were born again. Also, names of Irish and French derivation became particularly popular, even for parents with no roots in those cultures. Thus came thousands of Erins, Kevins, Brians, Seans, Shannons, Taras, Danielles, Michelles, and Nicoles. Other little girls were liberated from female stereotypes with onetime Upper-Class Gentleman Names, such as:

ASHLEY	DARCY
BLAIR	KIMBERLY
BLAKE	LESLIE
BRETT	LINDSAY
BROOKE	WHITNEY
COURTNEY	

At the opposite end of the scale were feminissima Victorian Valentine Names—Amanda, Jennifer, Jessica, Melissa, Samantha, Vanessa, and Victoria.

Big changes came in the eighties, the era of Yuppie-Gekko greed, Reaganomics, and Calvin Klein consumerism, when suddenly image was all. By the middle of the decade, solid, timeless classics had reemerged, with legions of babies named Katharine, Elizabeth, Emily (which would reach #1), William, Daniel, Andrew, and Christopher. There was also a different kind of naming equality than that seen in previous decades, providing both daughters and sons with Upwardly Mobile Androgynous Names such as the aforementioned Ashley—once one of those elegant, *Gone-with-the-Wind* gentleman's names—which enjoyed a meteoric rise for girls, reigning at number one for much of the decade. Others in this category include:

CARTER	PEYTON/PAYTON
DREW	PORTER
EMERSON	QUINN
JORDAN	SCHUYLER
KIMBALL	SLOAN
KYLE	SYDNEY
MALLORY	TAYLOR
MORGAN	TYLER
PARKER	

When the eighties and some of its more superficial values crashed, several of its naming trends survived, but with a nineties twist. The veneer of old money was replaced by a more solid and honest emphasis on genuine family history, with names that honored actual ancestors rather than those conjuring up phony WASP pedigrees. Ethnic names and surnames, as well as place names and nonglitzy family names, became more fashionable than the slick choices of the eighties, directions that have continued well into the new millennium.

And where are names trending today? For what's happening right now, see What's Hot, page 3.

> I was always irritated that my name was Jessica. Come on, it's a very eighties name, because there were tons of Jessicas in every school I went to. There's something great about having a unique name. It's part of your identity.
>
> —Jessica Alba on naming her daughter Honor

African-American Naming Traditions

On the very day that Barack Obama was elected, reports started streaming in from across the country (and around the world) of babies being named both Barack and Obama, and the craze shows every sign of continuing. There can be little doubt that this is an expression of ethnic pride in and excitement over the election of the first African-American president of the United States—and the first with an identifiable, authentic black name, marking the culmination, in a way, of the racial divide in baby naming.

There has been a separate black naming tradition in this country since the first slaves were brought to America and given distinctive names by their masters. Over the centuries, African-American names continued to evolve apart from white-American names via different ethnic customs, religious practices, geographic traditions, and the *Roots* phenomenon of the 1970s. The result: A lexicon of black names that's become only more separate from white names over time.

Early plantation owners renamed their newly arrived slaves, trading their African names for classical names designed to show off the owners' erudition. The slave masters, who in the beginning also named the slaves' babies, deliberately chose names that were not used for whites and that were also unique on the plantation. Slaves themselves tended to use their owner-imposed names when with whites and their African names or other nicknames among themselves.

Classical names from Greek and Roman mythology and history that accounted for one-fifth of the names given to slaves before 1800 include:

Female

CHLOE

CLEOPATRA/CLEO

DAPHNE

DIANA

DIDO

FLORA

JUNO

MINERVA

PHOEBE

SAPPHO

THISBE

VENUS

Male

ADONIS

AUGUSTUS

BACCHUS

CAESAR

CATO

CICERO

CUPID

HANNIBAL

HECTOR

HERCULES

JUPITER

NERO

PERICLES

POMPEY

PRIMUS

SCIPIO

TITUS

VIRGIL

In Colonial times, as many as 20 percent of the slaves in the Carolinas, for example, bore African names, most notably day names, which relate to the day of the week on which the person was born. The West-African day names, often translated to English cognates such as Judy for Juba or Joe for Cudjoe, are:

	Female	**Male**
Sunday	QUASHEBA	QUASHEE
Monday	JUBA	CUDJOE
Tuesday	BENEBA	CUBBENAH
Wednesday	CUBA	QUACO
Thursday	ABBA	QUAO
Friday	PHEBE/PHIBBI	CUFF/CUFFEE
Saturday	MIMBA	QUAME/KWAME

Names were also chosen that signified months of the year, seasons, and holidays. Some of these that have survived on the rolls include: Monday, Friday, Christmas, Easter, March, and July.

Place names, often signifying a site of importance to the slave owner, sometimes relating to one meaningful to the African-American parents, were also commonly used: As many as a quarter of male slaves received a place name in the mid-1700s. Among those found:

ABERDEEN	DUBLIN
AFRICA	GLASGOW
ALBEMARLE	LONDON
AMERICA	NORFOLK
BALTIMORE	RICHMOND
BARBARY	WILLIAMSBURG
BOSTON	WINDSOR
CAROLINA	YORK
CONGO	

Most avant-garde-sounding to our modern ears are the word names used for and by African Americans, signifying everything from the weather to virtues à la the Puritan naming traditions. Their use relates to the African belief in the power of a name to shape personality or influence fate or impart a certain quality—though many are far from uplifting. Some virtue and word names recorded among early African Americans are:

Female

CHARITY
DIAMOND
EARTH/EARTHA
HONOR
HOPE
JEWEL
LOVE
MOURNING
OBEDIENCE
PATIENCE
PROVIDENCE
QUEEN
TEMPERANCE

Male

CALIFORNIA GOLD
DUKE
FORLORN
GOODLUCK
HARDTIMES

JUSTICE
KING
LOWLIFE
MAJOR
MISERY
PLENTY
PRINCE
SQUIRE
SUFFER
VICE

Both

CHANCE
FORTUNE
FREEZE
LIBERTY
PLEASANT
RAINY
STARRY
STORMY

After 1800, most African Americans chose their own names, often naming children after grandparents, which served to extend a family's roots back to Africa. The other major development in the nineteenth century was the conversion of many blacks to Christianity, and their adoption of biblical names. Popular choices included:

Female	Male
DELILAH	ABEL
DORCAS	CAIN
ESTHER	ELIJAH
HAGAR	EPHRAIM
HANNAH	EZEKIEL
JEMIMA	HEZEKIAH
KEZIAH	ISAAC
LEAH	ISAIAH
RACHEL	ISHMAEL
REBEKAH	LAZARUS
RHODA	MOSES
TAMAR	NOAH
ZILPAH	SAMSON
	SHADRACH
	SOLOMON
	ZACHARIAH

In the mid–nineteenth century, free blacks in New Orleans began adopting the French-style "De" and "La" suffixes for babies' names, often indicating paternity that may have not been acknowledged by society at large. John's son, for instance, might become DeJuan. This form still flourishes among blacks today.

After abolition, many African Americans distanced themselves from names identified too closely with slavery: Pericles might have become Perry, Willie formalized his name to William. In the early twentieth century, black names and white names were as alike as they would ever be. Still, there were meaningful differences. A detailed survey of black female names in Augusta, Georgia, in 1937 shows many informal forms of names on the white popularity lists—Lillie instead of Lillian, for instance, or Janie instead of Jane—that reflected blacks' subordinate position in society. The most popular include:

ANNIE	LIZZIE
CARRIE	LULA
FANNY	MAMIE
HATTIE	MATTIE
JANIE	SUSIE
LILLIE	

Black and white naming patterns began to diverge sharply again in the 1960s and 1970s, with the rise of Black Nationalism and ethnic identity. The typical black girl born in a black neighborhood in California in 1970 was given a name that was twice as common among blacks as it was among whites, according to Levitt and Dubner's *Freakonomics*. By 1980, that baby would get a name that was twenty times more common among blacks. Still today, black parents are statistically more likely to choose a name that's one-of-a-kind. Other popular names among African-American parents relate to black celebrities—Tyra (Banks) and Jada (Pinkett Smith)—star athletes—Isiah (Thomas) and (Michael) Jordan—authors—Maya (Angelou) and Zora (Neale Hurston), and even the color black (Ebony and Raven). Some parents choose place names—Kenya, Nairobi—and the popular name Nia relates to the holiday Kwanzaa.

It's one thing if your name was Barack Smith, or Barry Obama, but Barack Obama, that's a killer, that's not gonna work.

—Barack Obama

MUSLIM & AFRICAN NAMES

Over the past decades many black parents have also looked to Muslim and African names for their children. Some favorites:

Girls
ADARA
AISHA
AKILAH
ALIYA
AMARA
ASHURA
AYANA
AZIZA
BARAKA (sure to rise
   in popularity)
BAYO
CALA
DALILA
FAIZAH
FAYOLA
HABIBAH
IMAN
ISSA
JAMILA
JINAN
KALIFA
KALILA
KARIMA
KATURA
LAILA
LATEEFAH
MARIAMA
MARJANI
NAJAT
NAYO
NEEMA
NYALA
RADIAH
RAJA
RAYYA
RAZIYA
RIHANA
SADIRA
SAFIA
SAHARA
SALIMA
SHANI
SHARIFA
TABIA
THANA
TISA
YASMEEN
ZAHRA
ZALA
ZALIKA
ZULA

Boys

AJANI
AKELLO
ALI
AMIR
AMJAD
AZA
AZIZ
BAHIR
BENO
FARRAN
HAJI
HAMID
ISHAQ
JABARI
JAMIL
JELANI
JIRI
JUMA
KALIQ
KAMALI
KARIM

KATO
KHALIL
MALIK
MANU
MASSAI
MORI
NAJIB
OJO
OKELLO
OMARI
RAFI
RAFIKI
RAMI
RASHID
SANYU
TABAN
TAMIR
TANO
ZAKI
ZUKA
ZURI

Ava & Aidan
Patron Saints of Popular Names

AND OTHER UNUSUAL, LIVELY, AND SURPRISING SAINTS' NAMES

If, because of tradition or religion you would like to give your child a saint's name, you don't have to settle for obvious choices like Anne, Elizabeth, Anthony, or Joseph. Yes, there really are Saints Ava and Aidan, as well as Saints Cloud, Conan, Olive, Zoe, and Hyacinth. What follows is a selective list of unexpected saints' names:

Female
ADELAIDE
AGATHA
ANASTASIA
AQUILINA
ARIADNE
AUDREY
AVA
BEATRICE
BEATRIX
BERNADETTE
BERNADINE
BIBIANA
CANDIDA
CLARE
CLAUDIA
CLEOPATRA
CLOTILDE
COLETTE
CRISPINA
DELPHINA
DIANA

ELEANORE	MADELINE
EMILY	MARCELLA
EMMA	MARINA
EUGENIA	MARTINA
EULALIA	MATILDA
EVE	MAURA
FABIOLA	MICHELINA
FELICITY	NATALIA
FLORA	OLGA
FLORENCE	OLIVE
FRANCES	PHOEBE
GEMMA	PRISCILLA
GENEVIEVE	RITA
GEORGIA	ROSALIA
GERMAINE	SABINA
GWEN	SALOME
HELENA	SILVIA
HONORATA	SOPHIA
IRENE	SUSANNA
ISABEL	TATIANA
JOAQUINA	THEODORA
JULIA	URSULA
JULIANA	VALERY
JULITTA	VERENA
JUSTA	VICTORIA
LELIA	VINCENZA
LOUISE	WINIFRED
LUCIA	ZENOBIA
LUCILLA	ZITA
LUCRETIA	ZOE
LYDIA	

Male

ABEL	DIEGO
ADRIAN	DUSTAN
AIDAN	EDMUND
ALEXIS	ELIAS
AMBROSE	EMIL
AMIAS	EMMANUEL
ANSELM	EPHREM
ARTEMAS	ERASMUS
AUSTIN	ERIC
BARDO	FABIAN
BARNABAS	FELIX
BARTHOLOMEW	FERDINAND
BASIL	FERGUS
BENEDICT	FINNIAN
BENNO	FLAVIAN
BLAISE	FLORIAN
BLANE	GERVAIS
BRICE	GILES
BRUNO	GODFREY
CASSIAN	GREGORY
CHAD	GUNTHER
CLAUDE	GUY
CLEMENT	HENRY
CLOUD	HUGH
COLMAN	IGNATIUS
CONAN	ISAAC
CONRAD	ISIDORE
CORNELIUS	ISRAEL
CRISPIN	IVES
DAMIAN	JOACHIM
	JONAH

JORDAN	PASCAL
JUDE	PEREGRINE
JULIAN	QUENTIN
JUSTIN	RALPH
KEVIN	RAPHAEL
KILLIAN	REMI
LEANDER	ROCH
LEO	RODERIC
LEONARD	RUFUS
LINUS	RUPERT
LLOYD	SAMSON
LUCIAN	SEBASTIAN
LUCIUS	SILAS
LUKE	SIMEON
MAGNUS	SYLVESTER
MALACHY	TITUS
MARIUS	TOBIAS
MAXIMILIAN	URBAN
MEL	VALENTINE
MILO	VINCENT
MOSES	VIRGIL
MUNGO	WOLFGANG
NOEL	YVES
OLIVER	ZACHARY
OTTO	ZENO
OWEN	

Jewish Names

So, what do we mean by a Jewish name? Is it one derived from Hebrew? An Old Testament name like Isaac? Is it a name with a Yiddish accent like Moishe? Is it one that has been used in the Jewish community for so long that it "sounds" Jewish, like Seymour? Is it a recently created name from Israel? Is it all or none of the above?

Just a few years ago, we felt comfortable asserting that there was no such thing as a "Jewish" first name anymore, but now we're not so sure. For although large numbers of Jewish parents continue to follow national trends, and there are as many Liam Spiselmans as there are Liam Fitzgeralds, growing numbers are now, like members of other ethnic and religious groups, looking back into their own heritage, at less-common Old Testament names, at Hebrew names, and at names that have become popularized in Israel.

Contrary to popular belief, there are no Jewish laws dictating that a baby be named after a deceased relative, and no reference to that practice in the Bible. In fact, names borrowed from the Old Testament did not come into use until the sixteenth century—before that each biblical personage, from Adam and Eve onward, was thought to have exclusive title to his or her name.

When masses of Jewish immigrants arrived at Ellis Island at the end

of the nineteenth century, most of them held on to a somewhat translit-
erated version of their original names. It was with their children, the first
American-born generation, when that suddenly changed. Following the
old tradition of using the same initial letter for the English name as for
the Hebrew or Yiddish one, and in an effort at instant assimilation, these
newcomers were determined to bestow upon their sons and daughters
the most elegant-sounding, nonethnic Anglo names they could find.
Thus, the sons of Moishe might be called Murray (a Scottish surname),
Morton or Milton (British surnames), Myron (a Classical Greek name),
or Marvin (Old Welsh). The strategy backfired, however, when these
names were adopted in such prodigious numbers that Milton, Marvin, et
al began to be thought of as "Jewish" names.

The names Milton and Marvin and their generational peers such as
Seymour, Stanley, and Sheldon are rarely given to babies today, and the
reason for this can be explained by the theory we call the Kosher Curve.
As we mentioned, first-generation immigrants typically try to renounce
any hint of their ethnicity by choosing the most mainstream names of
their new country. It isn't until the third or fourth generation that there
is a resurgence of ethnic identity and pride, plus sufficient distance for
the original names to sound fresh and youthful enough to be bestowed
on a baby. By the 1970s, the Jewish world was ready for a new era of
Maxes, Sams, Bens, Jakes, Mollys, Beckys, and Annies, while the eighties and nineties saw a rebirth of Annas, Hannahs, Harrys, Jacks, Sarahs,
Rachels, and Rebeccas, and the present generation is rediscovering the
vintage charm of such Bubba and Zayda names as Sadie and Sophie,
Isaac and Eli. If you're wondering if we're ready to bring back Bertram
and Bertha, the answer is—not quite yet.

HEBREW-ISRAELI NAMES

Here are some appealing names heard in Israel, both traditional Hebrew ones and those newly created there.

Girls	Boys
ADAH	ABBA
DALYA	AMOZ
DEVORAH	AVIV
DOVEVA	ELIAZ
KELILA	LEV
LEILI (LAY-Lee)	MALACHI
LILITH	ORAN
MARAH	REUEL
SARAI	URI
TAMAR	ZEV
YAEL	

THE KOSHER CURVE

Over the decades, American-Jewish names have shifted with the trends of the times. Here's how some representative first-generation names have morphed through the twentieth century and into the twenty-first.

ABE	ARTHUR	ALAN	AIDEN
BENNY	BERNIE	BARRY	BRADY
BESSIE	BETTY	BEVERLY	BETHANY
BLUMA	BLANCHE	BLOSSOM	BLAIR
CHAIM	HYMAN	HOWARD	HOLDEN
CLARA	CLAIRE	CARLY	CIARA
FANNY	FRANCES	FRANCINE	FRANCESCA

GOLDIE	GOLDA	GLORIA	GEORGIA
HERSCHEL	HERBERT	HENRY	HENDRIX
IDA	ADA	ADELE	ADELINE
ISAAC	IRVING	IRA	ISAIAH
JAKE	JACK	JASON	JACOB
JULIUS	JULES	JULIAN	JUDE
LEO	LEON	LEONARD	LIAM
LOUIE	LEWIS	LUTHER	LUCA
MAX	MACK	MAXWELL	MAXIMUS
MINNIE	MINA	MINDY	MIA
MOISHE	MORRIS	MAURY	RORY
NATHAN	NORMAN	NOAH	NORTH
NELLIE	NORMA	NELL	NEVE
RIFKA	RIVA	RICKI	RILEY
ROSE	ROSEANNE	ROSY	ROMY
SADIE	SALLY	SAMANTHA	SADIE
SOL	SAUL	SAM	SAWYER
SONIA	SONDRA	SANDRA	SAVANNAH
SOPHIE	SHEILA	SHARI	SOPHIA
TESSIE	THELMA	TERRY	THEA
WILLIE	WALLY	WARREN	WARD
YETTA	YVETTE	VIVIAN	VIOLET
ZELIG	ZACHARY	ZAK	ZANE

MIXED-MARRIAGE NAMES

If one of you is Jewish, and the other is not, you're probably already skilled in the art of compromise, maybe having both a minister and a rabbi at your wedding, or having a Star of David atop your Christmas tree. Now that you're expecting a baby, you want a name that has meaning in both your cultures, one that's traditionally been used by both Christians and Jews, a name that you'll both be able to live with.

Some of the names on the following list are classic Hebrew examples that have also been used by Christians: Daniel, for example, and David and Susannah. Others, while they may be English or French or Greek by derivation, have been well used by Jewish parents through the years. We've also included names that, though they may have been overused in recent years—Sarah, for example, and Benjamin and Samuel— nonetheless offer the requisite compromise. If you don't mind a name that's popular—or even prefer one—then Abigail or Ethan may satisfy all your criteria. If, on the other hand, you have a horror of giving your child a trendy name, consult also So Far In They're Out on page 35.

Of course, not every conceivable option is on this list. Depending on your religious feeling (and also, to some extent, your last name), you and your spouse may be comfortable using a name as goyish as Grace or as Jewish as Chaim—both perfectly sound names, but not included here, and nor are names as trendy as Taylor or as musty as Milton. So, here is a wide selection of names that afford a good compromise for parents in mixed marriages:

Girls

ABIGAIL
ABRA
ADRIENNE
ALICE
ANDREA
ANNA
ANYA
AUDREY
AVIVA
BEATRICE
BELLA
BLANCHE
CARMELA
CELIA
CHARLOTTE
CHLOE
CLAIRE
DAISY
DARA
DEBORAH
DINAH

EDEN	MARAH
EDIE	MARGO
ELEANOR	MARINA
ELLA	MAYA
ELLEN	MINNIE
EMILY	MOLLY
EMMA	NATALIE
EVA	NELLIE
EVE	NINA
FRANCES	NORA
HANNAH	PAULINE
HELEN	PAZ
HELENA	PEARL
HILARY	PHOEBE
JESSICA	RAFAELA
JILL	RAINA
JUDITH	RAMONA
JULIA	RAPHAELA
KYRA	ROCHELLE
LAILA	ROMY
LAURA	ROSIE
LAUREL	ROWENA
LEAH	SADIE
LEILA	SAM
LIBBY	SAMANTHA
LILA	SELA
LILY	SOPHIE
LYDIA	STELLA
MABEL	STEPHANIE
MACY	SUSANNA
MAE	SYDNEY

SYLVIA	GEORGE
TAMAR	GIDEON
TILLIE	GUS
TOBY	HARRY
TWYLA	HENRY
UMA	ISAAC
WILLA	JACK
ZOE	JAKE
	JARED
Boys	JEREMIAH
AARON	JEREMY
ABBOTT	JESSE
ABNER	JONAH
ADLAI	JORDAN
ALEC	JOSIAH
ARI	JUDAH
ASHER	JULIAN
BARNABY	LEO
BENJAMIN	LEVI
CALEB	LEWIS
CHARLIE	MALACHI
DANIEL	MARCUS
DAVID	MATTHEW
ELI	MAX
ELIJAH	MILO
ELLIOT	NATHAN
EMMET	NATHANIEL
ETHAN	NOAH
EZEKIEL	OREN
EZRA	OSCAR
GABRIEL	PAUL

PETER

RAPHAEL

REUBEN

SAMSON

SAMUEL

SASHA

SETH

SIMON

STEVEN

TOBIAS

ZAK

ZEV

ZION

In an interview with the *Jewish Journal*, Helena Bonham Carter confirmed that her and Tim Burton's baby daughter had been named Nell. Nell is named after "all the Helens in the family," Helena explained. The actress's mother was called Elena, and her maternal grandmother was named Helene. "I feel quite atavistic in the sense that I want them to know where they come from," the actress explained.

International Ideas

The globalization of the culture has introduced us to a whole world of exotic (to us, anyway) names—British chefs named Nigella on TV, Brazilian supermodels named Gisele on the runway. But that's just the tip of the iceberg: there are hundreds and hundreds of names we've never even heard of here, many of which are on their country's popularity lists. Here is a selection of what's currently in favor in Holland, France, Germany, Italy, Scandinavia, and Spain.

DUTCH NAMES

Girls

ALEENA
ANOUK
FLEUR
ISA
LIA
LOTTE
MARIELA
MEENA
ROMEE
SANNE

Boys

BRAM
DAAN
KEES
LARS
MILAN

SEM	THIJS (TICE)
STIJN	VAN
SVEN	

FRENCH NAMES

Girls	Boys
ANAÏS	CORENTIN
CAPUCINE	FLORIAN
FLAVIE	MAEL
LILOU	MATHIS
LOUNA	MAXENCE
MAELLE	RAYAN
MAEVA	ROMAIN
NOÉMIE	THIBAULT
OCÉANE	VALENTIN
PRUNE	YANIS

GERMAN NAMES

Girls	
ALINA	NEELE
AMELIE	PIA
EMILIA	
GRETE	**Boys**
JANA	FABIAN
JETTE	FLORIAN
LEONIE	FYNN
MAJA	JANNIK
	JONA

LUKA	OLE
MATHIS	TIMO
NIKO	

ITALIAN NAMES

Girls	Boys
ALESSA	AGOSTINO
AMEDEA	ALDO
AZZURA	ALESSANDRO
BIBIANA	BIAGGIO
CARMELA	BRUNO
CIARA	FRANCESCO
ELENA	LUCIANO
FRANCA	PAOLO
LUCIA	PIETRO
PAOLA	VICENZO

SCANDINAVIAN NAMES

Girls	THEA
ALVA	TUVA
ANNEKE	
BRIET	**Boys**
EIRNY	AAREN
LIVA	ANDERS
MAJA	ANDREAS
MALIN	FILIP
MALOU	IVER

JEPPE OLAV
MAGNUS SANDER
MATHIA

SPANISH NAMES

Girls	Boys
ADRIA	ÁLVARO
AINHOA	ARNAU
AITANA	CALIXTO (cah-LEEKS-to)
ALBA	GONZALO
ARIADNA	GUILLERMO
AROA	IKER
CANDIDA	JORDI
LAIA	ORIOL
NEREA	POL
ROCIO	ZENOBIO

Whose Name Is It, Anyway?

It is Thanksgiving. You and your sister-in-law, both newly pregnant, are sitting with the rest of the family around the table. The conversation turns to names.

"If we have a boy, of course he will be Charles the Third," says your sister-in-law, smiling sweetly at your father. Your brother, Charles Jr., beams.

You, on the other hand, choke on your cranberry sauce. Ever since you were a little girl, you've wanted to name your first son Charles. Besides being your father's name, it's also your husband's father's name, your brother's name, and your favorite name for a boy in all the world.

"We were planning on Charles, too," you manage to sputter.

"You can't have it," booms your brother. "Clearly, it's our name."

"There's room for two Charleses in the family," you reason. "We'll just use different nicknames."

"Fine," your brother says. "But we're not getting stuck with Chuck."

"Now, now," soothes your mother. "What if you both have girls?"

"Ava," you and your brother say in unison.

If you and your spouse have proliferating siblings, the issue of who gets to use which names is one you may have to face. And a difficult issue it is. Does a son have absolute dibs on his father's name? Is there room in a family for two cousins with the same name? Is there a pecking order for who gets traditional family names? Is getting there first a good enough reason to usurp somebody else's name? Can you set claims on a name to begin with?

How you answered these questions depends a lot on your individual family. In some families, the oldest son has eternal right to his father's name, even if he never has a son of his own. In other words, it's first-come, first-served, with the understanding that there will be no later duplications. And some families just play catch-as-catch-can and worry later about how they'll deal with three cousins named, say, Eric.

If you anticipate some name wrestling within your own family, keep the following tips in mind:

Announce your own choices early on: If you have an absolute favorite name you're sure you will use, don't make a secret of it. Planting it in everyone's mind as "your" name can help avoid problems later.

Don't steal someone else's name: We're not talking about naming your baby Letitia, unaware that, on the same day, in another state, your sister is naming her baby Letitia. We're talking about naming your baby Letitia when your sister has been saying since she was fifteen that her fondest wish in life was to have a little girl named Letitia. And your sister is pregnant. And knows she's having a girl.

Avoid carbon copies: Two little Caroline Townsend Smiths in a close-knit family is one too many. If you want to use the same first and middle names that a sibling uses, can you live with a different nickname—Carrie, for instance? Or can you vary the middle name, so that, at least within the family, one cousin is called Caroline Townsend and the other, say, Caroline Louise? The only case in which two cousins named Caroline Townsend and called Caroline can work is if they have different last names.

Honor family traditions: If the oldest child of the oldest child in your family is always named Nicholas, don't break rank, unless your oldest sibling is a nun, priest, or gay rights organizer who has formally renounced rights to the name.

Take unintended, unimportant duplications in stride: We know two sisters-in-law, living across the country from each other, who were pregnant at the same time: Jane due in January, and Anne in April. During their annual Christmas Eve phone conversation, Jane said she was sure she'd have a boy, and that they were planning to name him Edward. "That's our name," gasped Anne. "Too bad," Jane said blithely. After a few minutes of intense anxiety, Anne decided Jane was right. Neither had officially "claimed" Edward, nor was it a name with family significance. It would be as ridiculous to insist that Jane change her choice at the eleventh hour as it would be to deny her own son the name just so it wouldn't duplicate that of a cousin he'd see, at best, once a year. Besides, Jane favored the nickname Eddie, while Anne preferred Ted. PS: Due to mitigating circumstances, neither baby was named Edward. They ended up with Juliet and Josephine.

Sibling Names

When we published our first baby-naming book, *Beyond Jennifer &
Jason,* we introduced the idea of sibling names: that the names of your
second, third, and subsequent children should "go with" that of your
first. Not matchy-matchy names, like Kayla and Kyle. But names that
carried a similar style and image, that were complementary and yet distinct.

We don't think you have to limit yourself to a handful of specific
sibling names. Sure, Delaney sounds great with Finnian and Kennedy.
But it would also work as well with any one of hundreds of other options. As long as you understand the basic principle behind choosing
a sibling name—think of providing each of your children with
separate-but-equal birthday presents and back-to-school outfits and
you get the idea—you're well on your way to making the right choice.

Some examples from our experience that work: Jane and William,
for instance, and Max and Lily are both good pairings because the
girls' names are clearly feminine and the boys' names are clearly masculine. The styles are consistent—Jane and William are both classics,
while Max and Lily are fashionable and informal.

Two brothers we know whose names catch the right rhythm are
Felix and Leo. Both are saints' names that haven't been used widely in

recent years and have an appealingly offbeat quality. The *x* and the *o* endings provide different but equally unusual sounds for the two names, and they are further related by both being feline.

What happens with all the unisex names that are around today? If you name your son Hayden, which is getting increasingly popular for girls, can you name his sister the equally ambiguous Riley? We say yes. In fact going toward the middle for both siblings is a better call than naming your son Hayden and your daughter something elaborately feminine like, say, Gabriella. A boy Hayden would more compatibly have a brother named Brock than Robert, while a girl named Riley's sister might be better named Delaney than Delilah.

But Hayden and Eli, a traditionally male biblical name, might be equally compatible, as might Hayden and Laurel. And Riley could get along well with a wide range of boys' names from obvious choices like Conor or Declan to anything from the offbeat Inigo to the all-American Charley.

The point: Sibling name possibilities are wide and varied. Just as each child will surprise you with his all-new recombination of your genetic material and his unique personality, so, too, should each child's name reflect his individuality.

How far toward uniqueness is too far? When a child's name makes him seem like a member of a different family. If your first two daughters are named Angelina and Annabella, for example, a third named Sawyer would feel decidedly out of step.

Some rules to keep in mind about sibling names:

Consider sibling names when you're naming your first child. Though you don't have to name your entire family at once, you do want to consider whether your first child's name is going to work with names you might want to use for subsequent children. Your first choice sets the tone for the rest of the family.

Don't be cute. No rhymes, sound plays, precious pairings. Resist the impulse, for example, to name Daisy's sister Maisie, Darcy, or Lily.

Beware the same-initial trap. Back in the day, many parents gave all their children names that started with the same letter. While this practice is somewhat dated today, it can be an all-right way to create family unity, as long as you choose an initial that includes enough distinctive names that you like. The problem comes in when you name your first two sons Edward and Elliot . . . and then find yourself with Boy #5 and choices limited to Earl and Edgar. But then again, if you have Boy #5, you probably have bigger problems than what you're going to name him.

Do maintain consistency of style, image, sex, and tradition. Everything doesn't have to line up perfectly. But at least one or two factors should be consistent.

Consider sibling nicknames along with proper names. Here's one that even we didn't anticipate. One of us has children named Rory, Joseph, and Owen. And so what did their nicknames morph into over time? Ro, Joe, and O. Whoa! Sometimes even the experts can't cover every base.

DOUBLE TROUBLE

Twins offer a rare opportunity for parents to choose two related names at the same time, but also multiply the potential difficulties of sibling naming. With twins, it can be more tempting to use rhyme, sound play, and same initial names, but in our opinion pairings like Eddie and Teddy, Faith and Charity, or Nicholas and Nicole should be relegated to a time capsule.

While same-initial names that are clearly distinct from each other—Garrett and Grace, say, or Susannah and Simone—are okay, different-initial names consistent in style and tone are preferable.

Some celebrity examples that work: Brad and Angelina's Knox and Vivienne, Julia Roberts's Phinnaeus and Hazel, Patrick Dempsey's Sullivan and Darby, and Marcia Cross's Eden and Savannah. Although each of these sets of names is very different in style and feel, they all embody the qualities that matter most in twin names. Each name in the set is distinct from the other yet they make a harmonious pair—exactly what most parents would wish for the twins themselves.

Gender compatibility may be more important for twins than it is for siblings. One pair of starbaby twins whose names don't quite work as well as they should: Sean "Diddy" Combs's Jessie James and D'Lila Star. Both are girls, yet Jessie's name seems thoroughly boyish while D'Lila's is feminine to the point of frilly. Melissa Etheridge's twins are Johnnie and Miller—but unless you know their middle names, you wouldn't guess that Johnnie is a girl, Miller a boy. Such gender confusion seems needlessly, well, confusing.

Style consistency is also important. Most of the examples here work really well, from the traditional Lucy and John to the quirky Juno and Rex. The pairing of John and Juno would not be so sweet.

Twin Starbabies

AVA & GRACE, Mia Hamm & Nomar Garciaparra

BRONWYN GOLDEN & SLATER JOSIAH, Angela Bassett & Courtney B. Vance

CHARLIE TAMARA TULIP & DOLLY REBECA, Rebecca Romijn & Jerry O'Connell

COCO TRINITY & SAWYER LUCIA, Diane Farr

DARBY GALEN & SULLIVAN PATRICK, Patrick Dempsey

DEXTER HENRY LORCAN & FRANK HARLAN JAMES, Diana Krall & Elvis Costello

EDEN & SAVANNAH, Marcia Cross

EMME MARIBEL & MAXIMILIAN DAVID, Jennifer Lopez & Marc Anthony

FINLEY & HARPER, Lisa Marie Presley

GRACE & HENRY, Norah O'Donnell

JAID THOMAS & JAX JOSEPH, Gabrielle Beauvais-Nilon

JESSIE JAMES (f) & D'LILA STAR, Sean "Diddy" Combs

JOHN DAVID & LUCY ELIZABETH, Nancy Grace

JOHNNIE ROSE & MILLER STEVEN, Melissa Etheridge

JULIANNA TEX & HENRY BENJAMIN, Emily (Dixie Chick) Robison

JUNO & REX, Will (Coldplay) Champion

KNOX LEON & VIVIENNE MARCHELINE, Angelina Jolie & Brad Pitt

MATTEO & VALENTINO, Ricky Martin

NATALIA & SANTINO, Adam Carolla

PHINNAEUS WALTER & HAZEL PATRICIA, Julia Roberts

SIERRA & SIENA, Kurt Warner

THOMAS BOONE & ZOE GRACE, Dennis Quaid

WILL & JESSE, Wendy Wilson

Bad Advice?

As soon as you announce you're expecting a baby, everyone from your mother to your best friend to the waitress at the place where you eat your daily sandwich wants to talk about names. And why not? It's a happy topic, it's interesting, and baby names are a subject on which everyone has an opinion.

Oh right—that's why not.

Let's say that you and your partner in baby-having have agreed that, if the baby is a boy, you will name him Henry. You tell your mother-in-law.

"I had a great-uncle Henry," she says. Pause. "He drank."

You tell your best friend.

"Oh, no," she says. "Henry sounds like a nerd."

The waitress weighs in. "What do you want an old-fashioned name like that for? What about something more modern, like Hunter? Or Cannon?"

Before all these outside opinions, you thought Henry was a fine name; now you're not so sure. And even if you still like the name Henry, you don't want your child's grandmother to associate him with the family drunk, your friends to gossip about your bad taste, total strangers to dislike your child because of his name.

The trouble is that no matter what name you set forth, somebody isn't going to like it. And the more you open up the baby-naming discussion, the more lame name ideas you're going to have to field.

Online name discussions only complicate the advice issue further. Yeah, they're fun and a great way to build community while you're pregnant. And expanding your sources on names can help enlighten you to the pitfalls of some of your name ideas—There are three Savannahs in my daughter's nursery school class!—help you think of fresh ideas, and be a way to play with middle name and nickname alternatives.

But they can also add to the confusion, make you feel bad about names you hold dear, and just plain lead you astray.

How to handle baby-naming advice, bad and otherwise?

An increasing number of parents handle it by refusing to talk about it. "We have our name picked out, but we're not telling anyone till the baby's born," they say, sweetly but firmly. And that's certainly effective in warding off unwanted opinions and unfair pressure, yet it carries issues of its own.

It might be helpful to learn ahead of time, for instance, that Wyatt is far from your own personal discovery. That Rory (to cite a personal example) is frequently understood as Laurie, Gloria, and Marie—and that it causes a lot of people to exclaim, "But that's a boy's (or a girl's) name!"

Plus, sitting around talking about names can be one of the most enjoyable and enlightening experiences of expecting a baby. How to indulge without getting swamped by bad advice?

Before you take an opinion to heart, consider the source. Would you let this person choose a paint color for your house? Pick out your clothes? If not, you might want to discount their taste in names.

Invite friends and relatives and even strangers to come up with their own list of names, which can help you judge their opinions of your choice. Mom's taste might be too rooted in the fifties, a friend's too influenced by reality TV, and your four-year-old might only like such names as Bambi and Cinderella.

Take a hard line with relatives who try to pressure you into a family name that isn't to your liking. You're completely within your rights to tell Mom or Uncle Roger that, much as you appreciate their thoughts, the name is your choice and yours alone.

We now have "PEOPLE WHO ALWAYS HAVE TO SPELL THEIR NAMES FOR OTHER PEOPLE" merchandise. People with unusual names! Show your frustration at everyone else's spelling.

—Cafepress.com ad

The Riddle of the Middle

Middle names have moved from supporting players to costars in the naming scenario, with most parents today seeking a middle name with real substance and meaning.

For one thing, there's been a resurgence of the venerable tradition of using Mom's maiden name in that place for both girls and boys. Other family names, such as Grandma's maiden name, which might otherwise be lost to history, or the name of a favorite uncle might also be used in the middle: trendsetters Angelina Jolie and Brad Pitt gave both their twins family middle names. So this is the perfect place for that vintage name from your family tree that's just a little too far on the fusty side for first name use—say Caspar or Cornelia—or for the name of a place that has had special significance for you—the city where you and your spouse met or spent your honeymoon, be it Roma or the Carlyle Hotel.

It can also be a safe slot for a name you aren't crazy about but feel a certain obligation to use: to honor a beloved relative or friend whose name you don't really love, or to keep your baby's other parent happy. Or you might want to reference a cultural hero of yours—we've heard of babies with Lorca, Kafka, Kipling, Amadeus, and Zhivago in the second spot. Even older siblings can get into the act, having some middle name input—though you might have to contend with ideas like Shrek or Captain Caveman.

There are a couple of interesting new trendlets that we've noticed in this area. One is using a nickname in the middle place. For example, Amanda Peet gave her daughter Frances the middle name of Pen—which is short for her mother's name Penny—and other celebs have used such middle names as Hank and Pete, rather than Henry or Peter. It's a cute and adoptable idea, bringing both a kind of lightness and a sense of intimate familiarity with the namesake.

A more pervasive trend is that of using two (or more) middles, in the tradition of the British royals. One idea is honoring both grandparents, as Gwyneth Paltrow and Chris Martin did with their children Apple Blythe Allison and Moses Bruce Anthony. Soleil ("Punky Brewster") Moon Frye—herself no stranger to unusual names—called her daughters Poet Sienna Rose and Jagger Joseph Blue (yes, Jagger Joseph is a girl, which brings us to a gender alert—you might want to think about the safeguard of having at least one of your child's names identifying its sex). Other celebs have used three or more, including Stevie Wonder (Mandla Kadjaly Carl Steveland Morris), Heidi Klum and Seal (Johann Riley Fyodor Taiwo) and Mariska Hargitay (August Miklos Friedrich Hermann).

Of course, in show biz, excess is to be expected, and a couple of performers have gone over the top. Danny Bonaduce has a pair of kids named Count Dante Jean-Michel Valentino and Countess Isabella Michaela; Bono named his son Elijah Bob Patricus Guggi Q, while Meat Puppets lead singer/guitarist Curt Kirkwood walks away with the prize. His twins' names are evidence of a trend gone wild, bearing the multi-monikers Catherine Louise Saint Elmo Amelia Violet Elizabeth Presley and Elmo Isaac Dean Dylanger Samuel Sinbad Soul. Try fitting those onto a college application!

SINGLE-SYLLABLE MIDDLE NAMES

Okay, so you don't want to fall back on the previous generation's cookie-cutter Designated Middle Names—no Ann or Beth or Jay for your little one—but, perhaps because you have multisyllabic first and/or last names, you still like the idea of a short, connective, one-syllable middle name. Don't despair—there are plenty of interesting choices that move way beyond Lee and Lynn. Following is a list of ideas primarily for girls, though several can work for boys, too.

BAY	DREAM
BECK	DREE
BIX	DUFF
BLUE	DUNE
BLYTHE	EVE
BRIGHT	FAY
BROWN	FIFE
BRYN	FINN
CEIL	FLANN
CHAN	FLYNN
CHASE	GRAY
CLAIRE	GREER
CLAUDE	JET
CLEM	JEX
CLEVE	JOSS
COLE	JUDE
DAY	KAI
DOE	KANE
DOONE	KAY
DOT	KIT
DOVE	LAKE

LANE	PLUM
LANG	POE
LARK	PRU
LIGHT	RAE
LIL	RAIN
LIV	SCOUT
LUC	SLOAN
LUZ	SNOW
MAE	SPENCE
MAEVE	TATE
MAIRE	TEAL
MAME	TESS
MAUD	TRUE
NYE	WEST
PAX	WREN
PAZ	XAN
PEARL	ZANE
PINE	ZEN

STARSTRUCK MIDDLES

Here are some of the inventive middle names celebrities have used for their offspring in the past few years:

AERIN	Fred Savage
ANAÏS	Jacinda Barrett
ARIELA	Halle Berry
ASTER	Gilbert Gottfried
ATTICUS	Tom Dumont
BEAR	Anthony Kiedis

BEBOP	Michael ("Flea") Balzary
BLUE	Veronica Webb
BRAVERY	Talisa Soto & Benjamin Bratt
CALLIOPE	Patricia Arquette
CALVO	Jaime Pressly
CLAUDINELLE	Wyclef Jean
CLOVER	Tony Hawk
CRICKET	Amy Locane
CRIMEFIGHTER	Penn Jillette
DANBI	David Alan Grier
GABO	Milla Jovovich & Paul Anderson
GOLDEN	Angela Bassett & Courtney B. Vance
GYPSY	Drea de Matteo & Shooter Jennings
HALCYON	Lauren Ambrose
HANK	Sara Gilbert
HARLOW	Joely Fisher
HONEY	Kate Winslet, Jamie Oliver
HUCKLEBERRY	Kimberly Williams & Brad Paisley
ICARUS	Lucy Sykes
IOLANI	Lisa Bonet
JUSTICE	Jaceon Taylor
KIPLING	Kim Raver
LIRON	Christina Aguilera
LORCAN	Diana Krall & Elvis Costello
LUELLA	Travis Barker
LUNA	Joely Fisher
LYON	Kyle MacLachlan
MADONNA	Geri Halliwell
MARIBEL	Jennifer Lopez & Marc Anthony
MARS	Sofia Coppola
MAXIMUS	LeBron James

MONTEZ	Monica
MORIAH	Taylor Hanson
NESS	Kevin Nealon
NESTA	Lauryn Hill, Ziggy Marley
NOUVEL	Angelina Jolie & Brad Pitt
OLWYN	Stella McCartney
PEN	Amanda Peet
PETE	Naomi Watts & Liev Schreiber
PLUM	Moon Unit Zappa
RAIN	Brooke Burke
RAVELLO	Woody Harrelson
ROCKET	Tom DeLonge
SONG	Brett Scallions
STORY	Minnie Driver
SURA	Renée O'Connor
SWEETHEART	Tobey Maguire
TEX	Emily Robison
TRUE	Meg Ryan
TULIP	Rebecca Romijn & Jerry O'Connell
VONNE	Sharon Stone
WINTER	Nicole Richie & Joel Madden
ZENOBIA	Tina Fey

You Say Maria, I Say Mariah

WHEN COUPLES DISAGREE ABOUT NAMES

Most couples agree on whether they want kids. They often reach an easy accord on *when* they want them. Many even are like-minded on such sticky issues as where they'd prefer to raise their children, how they'd like to educate them, and what style of discipline they believe in.

Choosing a name can prove more problematic than any of the above.

Names are one of those subjects that summon up all kinds of hopes and fears, desires and secrets that you might otherwise never have guessed about your mate. How else, but on the hunt for the perfect name, would you discover that your husband once got his nose bloodied on the playground by a red-haired she-bully named Kelly, and ever since cannot abide the name? When might you have occasion to confess that you dated not one but, um, three guys named Michael, so that he might not want to push that one for your firstborn son?

Such individual associations are par for the baby-naming course. Conceiving your child may have made you feel, more than any other step you've taken together, as if you had finally and truly become one. Choosing its name can remind you that, nope, you're still actually two.

There are all those people with all those names that each of you knew and loved or hated before you met each other. Those ancient experiences and emotions are key determinants of whether you like a name or loathe it. If you and your spouse retreat to separate corners and draw up individual lists of your favorite names, chances are you'll cross off half of each other's picks because you went to third grade with an Elizabeth whose nose was always running, or had a college roommate named Daniel who told terrible jokes.

Then there are your individual families and backgrounds to consider. Couples who successfully negotiate religious differences and complicated family holidays sometimes find themselves stymied by conflicting name ideas and requirements. One couple we know, for instance, compromise his Jewish and her Catholic backgrounds by attending a Unitarian church, but when naming their baby hit a deep divide when he wanted to follow religious tradition and give their child a name that started with the same letter as that of his recently deceased grandmother, and she bucked against being pinned down to only names beginning with s. (See some Mixed-Marriage Names on page 186.)

Another factor that can make for difficult name negotiations between prospective parents is that, in most cases, one of you is a man and the other is a woman. A study by Charles Joubert of the University of Northern Alabama demonstrated that men and women often have very different tastes in and ideas about names.

Joubert asked his male and female subjects to choose a name for a hypothetical child from a list he provided. Men, he found, were more likely to choose common or old-dated names for children of either sex, and less likely to propose recently popular names. Women were more likely to propose a common name for a boy than for a girl, less likely to select unusual names for boys than for girls.

Another issue: Men and women often have very mixed ideas on the child's gender identity and on the signals a name sends out. Many moms, for example, like boys' names that sound creative and nontraditional, but some dads are fearful of giving their son a name that might label the boy as a wimp.

"There are two kinds of boys' names," one father told us, "the kind that makes you sound like you'd sit in the outfield looking at the clouds. I was the type of kid who looked at the clouds, but I want my son to be a ball-hitter." A Bob, in other words, or a Dave, or a Steve, or a Charlie. Not a Miles or a Jasper.

On the other hand, moms tend to be more comfortable with girls' names that are androgynous or even decidedly masculine, while dads seem to like frillier, more traditional girls' names. Mom campaigns for Alix, for example, while Dad favors Alicia; Mom likes Sydney, Dad opts for Samantha.

Why the gender gap? Some mothers may be more sensitive than their spouses to sexism and stereotyping. And for girls, moms tend to think about names they would have liked to have had themselves, while dads are looking at the issue from the outside in. Of course, when it comes to naming boys, the situation is reversed, and it's the father who can imagine firsthand what it might be like to be a Cyril when teams are being picked.

What of gay couples? There, the associations to names might be more similar, but the gender issues may get more complicated. A gay male couple we know who were adopting a baby daughter, for instance, wanted to give her the family name Carson. But, they worried (as did we), was it unfair to give a girl who was sure to face complex gender issues in her upbringing a name that further muddied the gender waters? Maybe, and yet this was probably the only child that they would have and they dearly wanted to use a name that had been in the family for generations. The solution? They named her Carson and call her the more conventional (and feminine) Carrie.

How to resolve any naming problems you and your spouse might be having? Here are some tips:

Talk about issues like image and gender before you talk about names. What do you each hope for in a child? Is your fantasy child energetic or studious, "all-boy" or gentle, feminine or tomboy? Coming to agreement on these matters, or at least getting them out in the open, can help when you're choosing a name, not to mention raising your child.

Rule out all names of ex-girlfriends and ex-boyfriends. No matter how much you like the name Emily, do not proceed with it if your husband had a long, torrid affair with an Emily way back when. Do not tell yourself you'll forget: You won't, and neither will he.

Make a "no" list as well as a "yes" list. Most couples only make lists of the names they like; it can help to make lists, too, of the names that are absolutely out for each of you. Include those you'd rule out for personal reasons (the roommate who stole all your clothes) as well as names you simply hate. Agree that neither of you will bring up the names on each other's "absolutely not" lists no matter how much you like them or how neutral they may be for you.

Avoid using the name-selection process as an opportunity to criticize each other's loved ones. When he campaigns for naming your son Morton after his father, this is not an excuse to tell him how much you dislike his father, no matter how much you detest the name Morton.

Investigate the reasons for each other's choices. Let's say you love a name your spouse hates. Instead of fighting over the name itself, explore what it is about the name that appeals to you. Figuring out whether you like a name because it's classic, or feminine, or stylish can lead you to other names with the same characteristics that both of you like.

Remember that parenthood is a joint venture. Just as your child will be a unique blend of characteristics from both of you, so should you endeavor to arrive at a name that combines each of your sensibilities and tastes. If you absolutely can't find a name you both love, agree that one of you will choose the first name, the other one the middle. Or, one will name this child, the other will name the next. Such enlightened negotiation and compromise is what marriage is all about.

THE ART OF COMPROMISE

Niki, the name we finally gave to our younger daughter, is not an abbreviation; it was a compromise I reached with her father. For, paradoxically, it was he who wanted to give her a Japanese name, and I—perhaps out of some selfish desire not to be reminded of the past—insisted on an English one. He finally agreed to Niki, thinking it had some vague echo of the East about it.

—Kazuo Ishiguro, *A Pale View of the Hills*

The Name Becomes the Child

Finally comes the day when you hold your live child in your arms and make a final decision on a real-live name. At that point, all the lists you've made, the considerations you've weighed, and the options you've juggled fall by the wayside, and you and your child are left with the ultimate choice.

What happens then?

Well, on the one hand, the struggle over Miranda versus Molly seems less crucial in the face of 3:00 A.M. feedings, colic, and the high cost of diapers. And it doesn't take long for your baby's persona to dominate the name, for your baby to become his or her name. For the first two weeks, you may find yourself still calling little Miranda "It"; for the next few, you may feel self-conscious each time you pronounce the name; but a month later you'll find that when you say "Miranda," you don't hear the sound of the name, but see instead your child's curved lips and dark curls.

On the other hand, once you've settled on a name, you deal with its myriad implications, often for the first time. You may discover, for instance, that your Aunt Elizabeth is not satisfied to be honored by a mere middle name, that people on the street do not necessarily assume that Riley is a girl, and that friends have to suppress a snicker when you tell them you've named your son Atticus.

This may not be fun. This may cause you to retrieve your original lists of possibilities and say to your spouse in the middle of the night, "Maybe we should have named him Jacob." And of course, it is possible to change a child's name two days or two months or even two years after you've given it, but it's not easy for many reasons, and it's not what we're considering here.

Better than contemplating a name change would be to mull over the fact that choosing one option—in names as in everything else—always means forgoing all others. That the name you've selected inevitably becomes influenced by reality, while the ones you've rejected remain fantasies, entirely pleasant because you alone control them. That in fact if you had chosen Jacob, say, you might then be worrying about its ordinariness, and wishing in the middle of the night that you had gone with something more distinctive, like . . . Atticus.

Obviously, much of the value of this book is that it helps you anticipate the real-world repercussions of a name. And much of the impetus for writing it came from our own experiences and those of our friends in choosing names for our children and living with those choices.

One of our friends, for instance, has two children, Emily and Jeremy. "When Emily was born we were living in the country and it seemed like a really special, unusual name," she says. "Then, when she was a few months old, we moved to the city, and I discovered that there were little Emilys everywhere. I felt terrible. I would listen in the playground for other kids named Emily, I would pore over nursery-school class lists for other Emilys, and if she was the only Emily, I would feel so relieved. On one hand, I feel badly because it seems as if the name is a cliché, but there also aren't so many Emilys as I'd originally feared."

Our friend pinpoints another reason why she was unaware of how widely used the name Emily was : "Having a first child, I didn't really know any other young parents. I had no idea what people were talking about when they named their kids or what the new style was. My idea of a trendy name was still Jennifer or Jason."

What then of Jeremy's name? "That one I haven't had so many problems with," she says, "except that some people keep trying to call him Jerry."

Parents who've chosen less-usual names talk of unanticipated problems with pronunciation and comprehension. A little girl named Leigh is sometimes called Lay; a child named Téa is called Thea by some people; Moriah is apt to be mistaken for Mariah.

Then there's the issue of the child's name vis-á-vis his or her looks or personality. Many parents wait to make a name choice until they see which of their finalists best fits the child. This makes some sense, but you should be aware that a newborn is not necessarily representative of the five- or twelve-year-old he or she will become. The chubby, noisy infant daughter you named Charlie may grow into a dainty, ultrafeminine ballet dancer, while the delicate baby who seems to be the quintessential Arabella may become, ten years later, goalie on the neighborhood hockey team.

This brings us to the flip side of the issue: Children can irrevocably color our perceptions of their names. You undoubtedly have unique feelings about certain names based on the children you know who bear them, and so do we. When we disagreed about whether to include a particular name on a list here, it was usually because we both knew people who brought different things to it: a handsome and irreverent Ralph, for example, versus a boorish one; an adorable kid named Kermit versus the frog on TV.

Reading this book can help prepare you for some of a name's eventualities then, but not for others. You wouldn't be surprised, as our friend was, that Emily is a fashionable name or that some people are bent on using undesirable nicknames. Neither will you be unaware of both the advantages and complications of giving your child a popular or unusual name, or that Cameron can be a girl's name, or that Atticus has an intellectual image, and so can be perceived by some people as a bit nerdy.

But no one, including you, has ultimate control over the person your child turns out to be. A name can remind you of your hopes and fears way back when childbirth was a point on the horizon, but your child—the one who's laughing or crawling or walking across the floor in his own special way—can remind you that Atticus by any other name, be it Jacob or Jehosephat, would still be your own sweet boy.

Index

Diana, 45, 128, 179
Diane, 128
Diantha, 39
Diaz, 121
Didion, 84
Dido, 16, 172
Diego, 53, 181
Diezel, 14
Digby, 48
Dijon, 56, 70
Dillon, 147, 152
Dinah, 38, 85, 102, 106, 128, 162, 187
Dion, 86
Dior, 81, 82
Diva, 16
Dix, 80, 113, 121
Dixie, 30, 32, 62, 106
Dixon, 92
Django, 86
Djimon, 17
Djuna, 83
D'Lila, 202, 203
Dmitri, 55, 89
Dob, 113
Doe, 211
Dola, 111
Dolley, 76
Dolly, 10, 30, 133, 202
Dolores, 111
Dolph, 140
Dominique, 96, 126
Domino, 10, 90

Don, 93
Donald, 164
Donatella, 81
Donegal, 56
Donna, 128, 166
Donnan, 50
Donovan, 63, 86, 120, 135, 147
Doon, 89
Dora, 74
Dorcas, 97, 175
Doreen, 100
Dorian, 88, 96
Doris, 128, 165
Doro, 111
Dorothea, 126
Dorothy, 74, 111, 128, 165
Dot, 30, 211
Douglas, 143, 166
Doutzen, 81
Dove, 44, 167, 211
Doveva, 185
Draco, 95
Drake, 44, 140
Draper, 20
Draven, 90, 141
Dream, 38, 211
Dree, 211
Dresden, 70
Drew, 8, 16, 31, 114, 116, 135, 147, 152, 170
Dries, 82
Dru, 152
Drum, 87

About the Authors

Linda Rosenkrantz is the author of several non-name books, including *Telegram! Modern History as Told Through More Than 400 Witty, Poignant and Revealing Telegrams* and the memoir *My Life as a List: 207 Things About My (Bronx) Childhood*; and coauthor (with her husband, Christopher Finch) of *Gone Hollywood* and *Sotheby's Guide to Animation Art*. In addition to contributing articles to numerous magazines, she writes a nationally syndicated column on collectibles. She lives in Los Angeles and named her daughter Chloe.

Pamela Redmond Satran, who has been collaborating with Linda Rosenkrantz on baby name books for more than twenty years, is also the author of four novels: *Suburbanistas, Younger, Babes in Captivity,* and *The Man I Should Have Married*. She cowrites the popular "Glamour List" column for *Glamour* magazine and contributes frequently to such publications as *The New York Times, The Huffington Post,* and *The Daily Beast*. Pam lives with her husband and three children—daughter, Rory, and sons, Joe and Owen—near New York City. You can visit her Web site at www.pamelaredmondsatran.com.

Please visit their baby name Web site at www.nameberry.com.